The
ART *of*
ILLUSION

The ART of ILLUSION

A Trompe l'Oeil
PAINTING COURSE

JANET SHEARER

NORTH
LIGHT
BOOKS

Contents

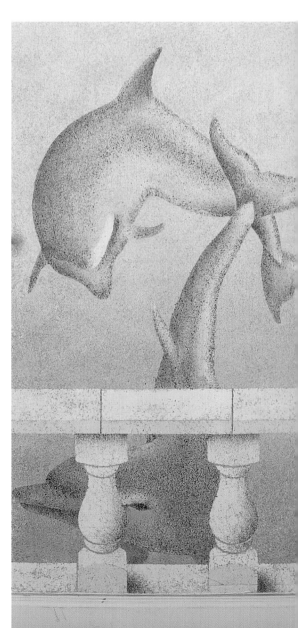

The Projects

Introduction

We can trace the history of murals right back to when cavemen drew and painted on the rough walls of their dwellings. They described the animals and nature that surrounded them with tremendous anatomical accuracy, scratching on to the rock, rubbing color from ground minerals into the scored marks. There isn't room in this book to do justice to a history of this type of painting. It's a fascinating subject in itself because we have recorded lifestyles, cultures, wars and rituals, not to mention extraordinary religious events. We are fortunate that these paintings have been preserved all over the world, in tombs, religious buildings and even those earliest of homes.

Although the Greeks may have invented trompe l'oeil, it was the Romans who developed it from ordinary decorative painting in order to increase the feeling of space in a room. By using theatrical architecture they created extraordinary illusions to adorn bare walls.

Translated from French, trompe l'oeil means "trick the eye," and although it really is just a visual joke, the joke is only effective if you do it well. That is what this book will teach you.

The wonderful thing about trompe l'oeil is its ability to change our surroundings and bring a little fantasy into our lives. On a gray winter's day, a painting like this can add warmth and color to a room, leading your eye out through the wall to far-off places (in this case, Tuscany).

Cheering up a rather plain pine fireplace can be fun if you've got time and patience! This one was first painted to look like marble, then I "inset" some "mosaic" panels which were copied from an amazing fireplace seen in a very impressive house.

Trompe l'oeil distinguishes itself from ordinary decorative murals by its intent to deceive, and it is this which sets it apart from ordinary still-life painting. The artist's technical skill is meant to go undetected and, with the use of perfect perspective, cleverly observed light and realistic colors, the trick is to make the onlooker believe that a flat surface is not actually flat, or that a space exists where there is no space. A trompe l'oeil painting is one which shows apparently three-dimensional objects and spaces in a way the eye accepts as realism in the context of their surroundings.

So why paint a trompe l'oeil?

The answer is simple: for fun! Human beings love to use their powers of observation to record lifestyles, longings, cultures and social trends. We have an innate sense of decoration and will always want to use whatever materials we can to enhance our surroundings. What is especially interesting is that we use trompe l'oeil and murals as a statement of permanence—a mark of identity, part of the architecture—and I hope to encourage you to try this in your own home.

We love color, texture, humor and illusion. Painting a mural means using them all. We like to change walls from the bland, bare anonymity of a single color to tell a story. Once a mural exists on a wall, that plain surface is lost, changed into another world in another dimension.

Nowadays too many of us have lost confidence in our own creative abilities because we don't believe we can match the expertise of professional artists. While I don't deny the magic and mystique that some people are fortunate enough to be born with, the skill to draw and paint well can be learned and, given a little practical guidance, anyone can do it!

My motivation for writing this book has been witnessing at first hand, during my short time of teaching, the pleasure people experience when they realize they can achieve the painting they have pictured in their mind because they have been shown how to. Unleashed into a fantasy world of make-believe, released from the confines of diminutive works of art, and maybe at the same time escaping from humdrum buildings, you can, with a bit of sensible help and advice, develop your own ideas into the most wonderful illusions.

How to learn

During the three years that I have been inviting people to join me for a five-day introduction to mural painting, I have seen spectacular results. People have come from all over the world hungry for knowledge. I now know with absolute certainty that if you have the skill to write your name, then by cultivating your powers of observation you can learn to draw and then to paint.

I put together the course on which this book is based, firstly deciding on an idea, developing it into a workable design drawn to scale, introducing the use of perspective, preparing surfaces, assembling materials, and finally the magical experience of putting the design on to the wall using the confidence gained by understanding how to do it and marveling at the unlimited versatility of the paint!

My objective has always been to furnish visitors to my studio with the skill to attempt a mural of their own, while making it clear that to become a master of this art takes much longer than five days and requires dedication, perseverance and a great deal of patience.

Anyone can do it!

I never intended to paint murals. I loved to paint "big" and came from a very creative family where this sort of behavior was acceptable. After art college, where I studied fine art but lost confidence as a painter, I became a photographic model in the fashion and advertising industry, which led me into the world of film and television, and introduced me to set-building. It was fast, efficient and exciting and it taught me that only the essentials are important when producing an effect.

Seduced by the excitement of film-making, I became, in quick succession, a stylist responsible for choosing props, a set-dresser, then a bona fide member of the Associated Cinematographic and Television Technicians, and worked my way up to Art Director. This was when the big change happened.

I had designed the set for a television commercial for a bank, employing a scenic artist to paint a bird 10 meters (11 yards) in diameter, typical of the bank's logo, on the studio floor. To my horror, I noticed after his departure that the bird's wings were wrong! I decided to repaint it myself overnight. When the film crew arrived in the morning, no one knew what had happened. My delicate reputation as a junior art director was safe, as was the reputation of the scenic artist. What had also happened, though, was a revelation to me. I had had more fun doing the painting than watching someone else do it!

Over the next few years I became a scenic artist with the help and guidance of Ken Hill, a master of the art, and his wife Nina, also an amazing painter. I learned how to paint enormous cloths with less effort than you would imagine, how to be economical with painted statements by understating something, and by making suggestions of forms rather than describing them in detail. I mastered the mixing of color and how to use color effectively to give the impression of realism. I learned about eye-levels in relation to the camera height. I tackled perspective, light sources, how to paint trees and grass, sky, clouds, buildings—you name it, and Ken had a method of dealing with it.

My first trompe l'oeil

The turning point for me came when someone connected with the film industry asked me to paint a mural around an indoor swimming pool in London's Hyde Park Square. The glass roof was two floors above the pool and all the walls were to be included in the design. Although I had a young baby at the time, I accepted the commission, taking on an assistant who painted and changed diapers when required. Sophie and I painted that trompe l'oeil under the most impossible conditions. However, the finished work was extensively photographed and was responsible for my launch into the world of mural painting.

After that, mural commissions came thick and fast. I have painted walls and ceilings in restaurants, pubs, hotels and private houses in the UK and abroad. Some of the larger commissions included a trompe l'oeil at Heathrow Airport's Terminal Three, two at Mormon temples, a huge single panel for the town of Tavistock in Devon, and the whole wall of the main bar on board the *Oriana*, one of the world's largest cruise liners. Each project brought its own upheavals, problems and challenges. The final results have always brought both relief and satisfaction for myself and, I hope, for my clients. And the thrill of looking at the blank space on the wall before I start has never left me.

Painting a mural to satisfy your own natural sense of decoration is an achievable goal, and great happiness can be found in the pursuit of achievable goals! Try it!

This was my first trompe l'oeil. At the time it seemed quite small compared with some of the film scenery I had been painting, but actually it was two floors high! The original glass roof was later replaced, which unfortunately cut through the top of my painted arch, as you can see here.

Design and Perspective

Designing your own trompe l'oeil is as important as painting it. Something has motivated you to make this huge statement. What is it? Perhaps your room has started to feel claustrophobic and you long to burst through into a panoramic landscape you once knew in Tuscany. Perhaps you yearn for a classical grandeur that you could never afford in your tiny basement apartment. Perhaps you have seen a beautifully painted trompe l'oeil in a restaurant and would like to have one yourself, or maybe you just want to make a small visual joke—putting your own stamp on the place you call home. It's your sign of permanence. It's your sign that you intend to stay there.

All murals have a reason for their existence. In this case, I wanted to keep a little bit of summer in our house right by the kitchen sink. Even in the middle of winter it makes us all feel warmer and brighter, and the flowers seem almost as fresh as real ones. This project is shown in more detail on page 94.

Gathering Ideas

How on earth do you start? Take a long, hard look at the room in question. Look at the furniture, at the existing architectural features and at the main light source. Think very carefully about your main viewpoint (by this, I mean the place from which you most often will be seeing the painting). When you start to put your ideas down on paper, you need to consider where you are standing in the room.

Try to visualize your inspiration in the context of the room. You may at this stage only have a "loose concept," but that's okay. Few of the great artists would know what to do without further hesitation. They would do exactly what you are going to do—retire to a comfy armchair with a huge pile of magazines and books featuring plenty of photographs of interiors and landscapes. Start to browse, keeping your original idea vaguely in your mind. Soon you will notice that you spot things relating to your own idea—the open window, that emotive Tuscan hillside, the French shutters you remember from your last holiday. All these should be marked, either with efficient sticky pieces of paper or with torn strips of newspaper. Gradually you will find your original idea blossoming, becoming more elaborate. You may even find that your early thoughts change and you discover something much more exciting. Keep your mind "open". I have often completely changed direction, and my first thoughts have been swept away after a couple of hours of serious browsing. This is called "sourcing" and may extend to books on architecture, African wildlife, gardening, history and so on. A visit to the local library may well be required. All the time, keep your intended wall space fixed firmly in your mind.

When you find something that interests you, you may like to make a drawing or tracing of it as well as marking the page in the book. It is very unlikely that you will find what you want in just one photograph. You may have that wonderful snapshot taken at dawn on your honeymoon in the Swiss Alps, but you need a foreground window to frame the beautiful view, and that may be found in a magazine photo. You may end up with a lot of tracings of different sizes, but don't be alarmed! There is a simple method for enlarging and reducing drawings that requires little more than the ability to work out simple proportions (see page 50). Layout or tracing paper is cheap, and at this stage you can afford to do as many sketches as you like—a lot less costly than making enormous mistakes on the wall.

Gathering ideas for a mural is like making a collage of things which interest you and which you can somehow include in your project. Magazines are an excellent source of material, especially if you don't mind tearing them up. Keep everything you find in a folder with all your doodles and sketches.

What you are looking for is an idea that works in the space you have available. If you are considering enlarging the room visually by leading the onlooker out through an apparent opening in the real wall, you must consider that the wall itself is the picture plane and the opening starts on this plane. Everything that is painted on this surface, as it were "in the real world," will be life size, but as the eye is led through the opening into the imagined space, the composition is affected by perspective.

Don't expect to get it right the first time. If you have trouble drawing something and are getting proportions wrong, turn it upside down to copy it. When an image is upside down, visual clues don't mean the same as when they are right-side up. Your brain won't recognize the picture, but if you slowly work your way through the drawing, from top to bottom, looking at the angles and lines, and the way they join up like a jigsaw, you will be amazed to find that it is easier to copy something this way.

Use every means at your disposal to expand your idea. Obviously, a camera is a marvelous tool, and if you can't find what you are looking for in someone else's photos, try to set up what you want yourself, and use the best equipment that you can to photograph your subject. When you photograph something, consider at the outset your eye-level (see page 17) and your light source (see page 29). This means that it helps to take the photograph of your subject from exactly the same height in relation to the subject as your viewpoint in the painting will be, rather than trying to adapt the drawing later.

If video cameras and computers appeal to you, use them. There are no limitations or rules to the process of designing a mural. It's relatively easy to "freeze" a frame on a video if you've got the right equipment.

By now you will have a pile of ideas strewn around you. Well-known and successful artists can take weeks to make up their minds about something, so remember it is no good rushing into a weak design.

Turning Ideas into a Painting

Even if the subject you have chosen to paint doesn't appear to have any perspective, believe me, it has, and you will find this chapter of the book useful. Perspective is not something you add at the last minute. In fact, it's impossible to draw anything at all without understanding it. But don't be afraid of it either.

Lighting Murals

Lighting has to be considered right at the outset of a project, and provision must be made for electricity cables to be laid where required (this may mean channelling in the wall to be painted). A uniform lighting system works best, because when you try to enhance the light artificially it can spoil your effect. It's also fatal to mix real architectural features with painted ones as the real ones cause lighting problems and unwanted shadows.

The information in this chapter applies to people working at different levels. You may find that for your first project you don't need to know about projections from plans and elevations, but knowing something about viewpoints, eye-levels and vanishing points does help.

I have shown here some perspective problems that were particularly relevant to the design of the mural of the Tuscan View. This trompe l'oeil painting was created as part of a kitchen wall, the idea being to show doors opening on to a sunny patio, overlooking a hillside in Italy with distant mountains shimmering in the heat (see finished painting on page 16 and page 55).

Discovering perspective for yourself

To have a better understanding of perspective and be able to turn your sketched ideas into convincing illusions, all of the following pages are relevant, but it will be useful for you to try one or two simple visual tests for yourself to understand the drawings shown here.

The first thing to establish when painting a mural is from where in the room you will most often look at the painting, that is, the main viewpoint (see page 16). This is always important, but particularly in the design of something like this Tuscan View, when the width of "view" visible, and the perspective of the foreground architecture need to be considered. In general, one stands centrally to look at a painting. When looking at a view through an opening, you see more of it close to the opening than you do if you take a few steps back (try doing this with a door or a window). Sometimes we have to pretend we are standing further away than we actually are able to in the room in order to minimize distortion.

Having chosen the viewpoint, the next thing to consider is the eye-level—your eye-level (see page opposite). This is something you need to

Establishing the Main Viewpoint

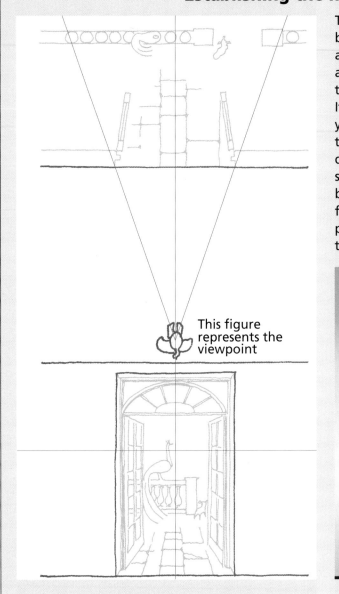

This figure represents the viewpoint

The first thing to establish is the main viewpoint by considering the most important place to look at the mural. When you look at a "view" through an opening, you see more of it if you stand close to the opening than if you take a few steps back. It helps to imagine a bird's-eye view of the wall, your viewpoint in the real world and a plan of the imaginary elements as shown in the top drawing. Underneath is the view as you want to see it on the wall, based on sketches which have been done freehand, but you now need to formalize the drawing. Below is the finished painting showing how important these first thoughts are.

KEY
- Black lines: *elements in real life, including edges of painted "opening"*
- Red lines: *eye-level*
- Blue lines: *imaginary elements*
- Green lines: *important "construction" lines*

master for all paintings. A few simple experiments can help you understand how it works. A good way to understand it is to hold a pencil horizontally at arm's length in front of you at eye-level and practice noticing where it is in relation to objects you are looking at—a landscape or the interior of a room.

The position of the eye-level determines the shape of all the elements in your painting. It can best be thought of as an imaginary line encircling you at the level of your eyes. If something you are looking at is below your eye-level, its shape will be affected accordingly. If you look up to your subject you will be seeing it differently. To achieve realism in your mural, you must think about where you are in relation to your subject.

When you are looking through magazines for ideas, it is a good idea to try guessing the position of the camera that took the photo. The eye-level is also the horizon in a flat landscape, but so often the actual horizon is obscured by trees, buildings or mountains, which might rise above the eye-level.

There are many visual "experiments" you can try without much effort. Try to stand in the middle of a (quiet) straight road, as shown on page 18, and assess the angle between the side of the road and the horizon. If you have any problems judging angles, try looking at them through a clear plastic protractor, making sure that the base line of the protractor is lined up with the horizon (you will have to hold the protractor upside-down).

Positioning the Eye-level

The eye-level is the imaginary line in front of your eyes which can be best understood if you hold a pencil horizontally at arm's length in front of you and practice noticing where it is in relation to a landscape you are looking at, or to the interior of a room (Fig 1). Also try seeing what happens to the shape of objects around you in relation to the pencil you are holding in front of you when you sit down or stand on a chair (i.e., what happens to the lines that form the edges of objects when compared with the horizontal line formed by the pencil).

For all my designs, I use a measurement of 1.5m (5') from the ground line (i.e., my feet) to my eye-level as a standard height and this level is always shown in red on the diagram. In the drawing above (Fig 2), having worked out my viewpoint I now need to establish the eye-level for the project. Try to

imagine whether you would look up to your subject or whether it is lower than your own eye-level, like the little dog shown here.

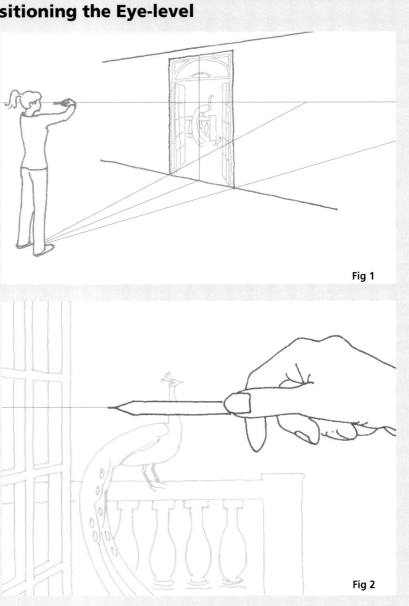

Fig 1

Fig 2

During your "experiment" you will have noticed that the sides of the road definitely seem to converge to a point at your eye-level. This is called a vanishing point and it is also important to be aware of this while designing a mural as, again, it affects your drawing.

All lines that are parallel to the direction of view (pointing in the same direction as your feet as you face your subject—in this case the picture plane) appear to converge to a point at natural eye-level. So far, we have simplified this to mean only the sides of a straight road if you are standing in the middle of it, but paintings would be rather boring if we just looked at straight roads or paths, so have a look at pages 19 and 20 to see how vanishing points may affect a more complex subject. In real life,

objects are not always conveniently placed with sides that are parallel to the direction of view, so artists can be helped by understanding what happens when the object you are looking at is set at an angle to the direction of view.

Going back to the scene we set before (i.e., standing in the middle of the straight road), a building set at an angle to the road will have two sides visible, the edges of which appear to converge to different vanishing points not in the center of the view. The important fact here is that these points still lie on the natural eye-level. It's possible to "eyeball" (i.e., to guess the position of) these other vanishing points approximately by throwing out an arm in a direction parallel to the sides of the building and then pointing to the eye-level as shown in

Picture Plane

The picture plane is the name given to the surface on which you intend to paint (or draw). This is perhaps best imagined as an enormous sheet of clear glass on which you have traced the image you see through it (Fig 1). In this book the picture plane means initially the paper on which you have designed the project (the scale of the image having been reduced) and then the wall or panel on which you paint (in which case the image may appear the size you have observed it to be).

All the elements that are affected by perspective and that in the end appear on the picture plane are drawn in blue. Black lines that appear on the picture plane have not been affected by perspective—these mark the outer edges of the painting.

If you can find a quiet, straight road, stand in the middle of the road and look straight ahead of you, holding a pencil horizontally at arm's length at your eye-level (Fig 2). You will notice that the sides of the road appear to converge in the distance at your eye-level.

You may also be able to judge the angle between your pencil and the sides of the road. Learning to judge angles like this will help you to draw.

Try imagining now that you have an enormous sheet of glass in front of you (as shown in the diagram) and could place the horizon at your eye-level as a horizontal straight line. If you could draw the side of the road on the glass, you have already begun to appreciate and understand the relevance of perspective in design.

Fig 1

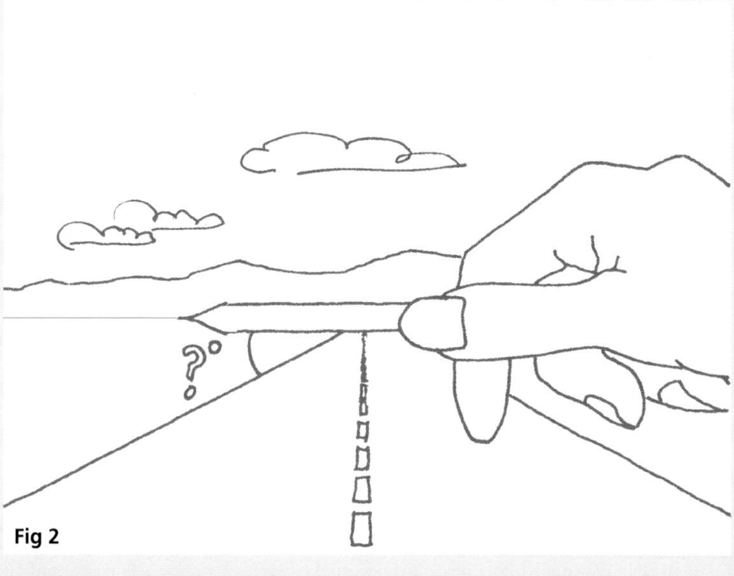

Fig 2

KEY
- Black lines: *elements in real life, including edges of painted "opening"*
- Red lines: *eye-level*
- Blue lines: *imaginary elements*
- Green lines: *important "construction" lines*

the drawing. If you had a sheet of glass placed in front of you, you could theoretically mark these vanishing points on the eye-level. Because buildings are cubes, there would be one vanishing point in a direction parallel to one side and another in a direction parallel to the other side, both being located at eye-level. Finding vanishing points can be done in a technical way by using the projection method to make a plan (see page 24).

After you have made yourself aware of all these ideas, you might be forgiven for wondering why they are relevant, but now you can use all of this knowledge to make a proper drawing in preparation for your mural. It is almost impossible to keep the painting under control on a large scale without first planning your design on paper. When you do start to paint, you will know exactly where you are on the wall.

Central Vanishing Point

All lines parallel to the direction of view appear to converge to a point on your eye-level. Try this with a straight road. If you are lucky enough to have found a road flanked by buildings, or a fence or indeed anything constructed with edges parallel to your feet (as you look along the road), you will notice that all lines parallel to your feet appear to converge at this one central point in the middle of the horizon, i.e., at your eye-level (Fig 1). This point is known as a central vanishing point.

In the case of buildings, the edges parallel to your feet form only part of a line to this point. Lines that are vertical stay vertical, and horizontal lines perpendicular to your own direction of view stay horizontal. If you do not have access to a long straight road, try standing in the middle of a reasonably uniform room. Face one wall, square-on and in the middle of it. Notice that the lines that form the edges of the floor and ceiling and that are parallel to the direction of your feet also appear to converge at an imaginary point on the wall facing you (Fig 2). To check this out, hold some long straight sticks in front of you and adjust the angle until they appear to follow the edges of the floor and ceiling to a meeting point in the middle of the facing wall. This is the vanishing point for these lines if we were to draw them on the picture plane. The photo of The Arches on the left shows how important vanishing points are in making an illusion work. For the methods used here, see pages 122-125.

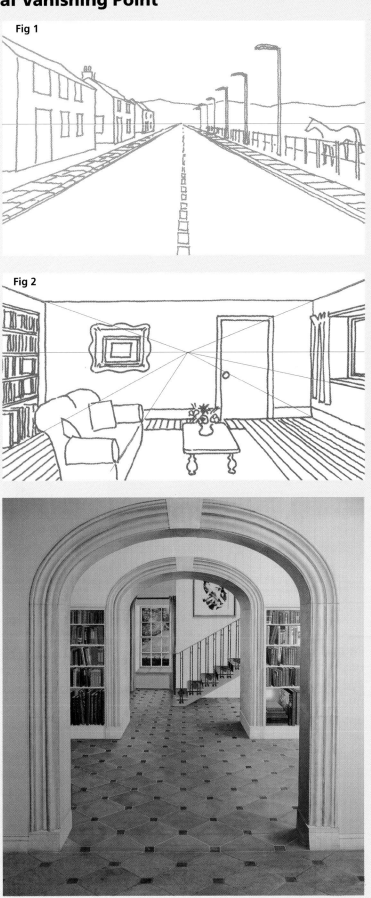

Fig 1

Fig 2

One-Point Perspective

The bird's-eye view (or plan) shows that we have chosen a point, usually dead center, to view the painting. From this viewpoint, all lines that would be parallel to the direction of view (i.e., parallel to your feet) appear to recede to a central vanishing point on the eye-level. This helps to make the corners of the opening look convincing.

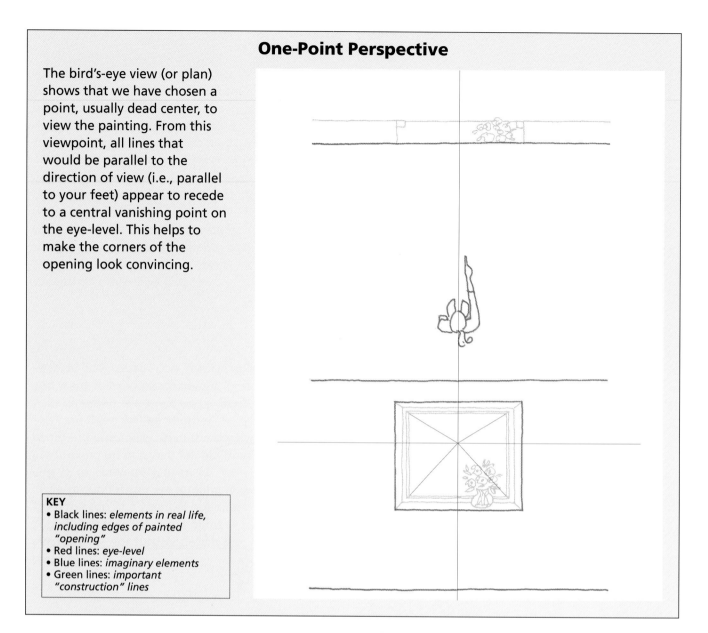

KEY
- Black lines: *elements in real life, including edges of painted "opening"*
- Red lines: *eye-level*
- Blue lines: *imaginary elements*
- Green lines: *important "construction" lines*

across the shape to show the eye-level. This you can measure in the scale you have chosen from the ground line. I usually use a scale of 1:10 or 1:20. Now fit your ideas into the space, considering whether you intend to look down on or up to things.

Once you have the shape of the wall to scale on paper, overlay pieces of tracing paper to maneuver the various elements into position, starting with the "opening," if there is one, through which you wish to look at the "view."

Do you want buildings to seem close or far away? When drawing any building in the distance be aware of your relationship to it. For example, if you are on level ground looking at a building in the distance, your eye-level will appear to be about two-thirds of the way up a ground-floor doorway in that building. This will help you to locate the building.

Using Vanishing Points

Now you can start to use vanishing points in your design. Lines drawn towards vanishing points on the figures appear in green as these are the "construction lines."

One-point perspective
One-point perspective is when we have just one vanishing point—often all you need for a good trompe l'oeil painting. This means we have chosen a point—usually dead central on the natural eye-level—to which all lines that would be parallel to our own feet as we face the picture plane appear to recede. This might mean lines forming the corners of an opening (e.g., a window or a door), or the upper and lower edges of books on a shelf (see page 128).

Try this on a drawing, adding in the shape of the wall and the eye-level (to scale). Then,

Two-Point Perspective

Again, in the bird's-eye view (or plan) we have a central viewpoint. Although we still need the central vanishing point for the corners of the opening, this time the open window has a vanishing point of its own, which we can "eyeball" by pointing in a direction parallel to the open window. The vanishing point for the open window will be found on the eye-level in the direction we pointed. This is called two-point perspective. The top and bottom edges and glazing bars of the open window appear to converge at this point. Finding these vanishing points in a more technical way is described on page 24.

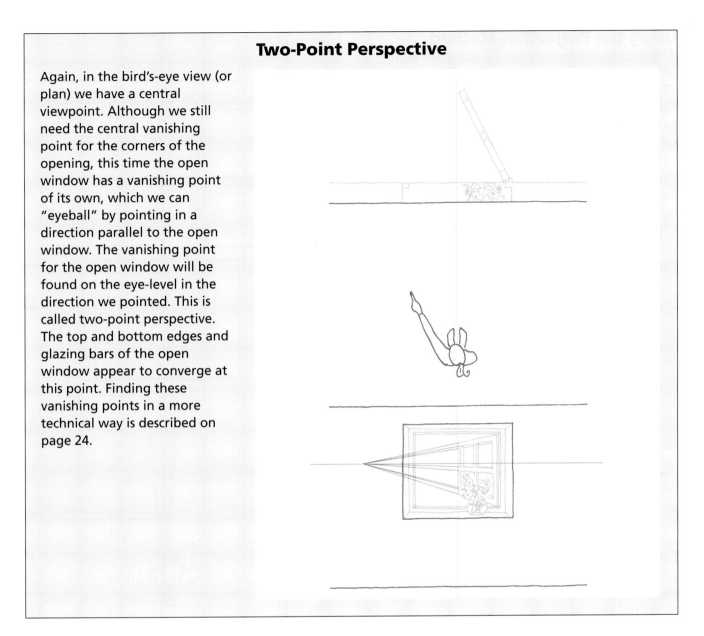

choose a point central to your viewpoint, and, using a ruler, draw the lines representing the corners of an opening so that they point towards this vanishing point. You will be truly amazed at how whatever you are drawing begins to make sense. It gives the drawing a feeling of depth, which can be observed in the Tuscan View (page 54), A Cornish Window (page 94) or The Arches (page 118).

Obviously, as you look at a recess containing a door or window, the upper and lower corners will have different angles when pointing towards a central vanishing point as the angles are affected by your eye-level. It's these differences that are important to the illusion.

Two-point perspective

A design will have more than one vanishing point (this can be seen in the "experimental" drawings on page 20) when you wish to represent objects set at different angles to the direction of view (which can be seen in the diagram above), where you might wish to show an open window, or open doors as in the Tuscan View painting (see page 54). The plan and elevation drawings on this and the page opposite show the difference between one-point and two-point perspective.

Three-point perspective

If you want to exaggerate the height of a building you are looking up at by making the vertical lines go to a vanishing point high in the sky—or conversely by making it seem as if you are very high up by making lines go towards a vanishing point deep underground—then you are drawing three-point perspective. This is shown on page 20.

"intuitive" sketch to make this decision. You will soon discover that standing very close to an open door produces very acute angles between the door frame and the top and bottom of the door. If your protractor is transparent, you can measure this angle by looking at it through the protractor itself. You can then compare this with the angle you sketched. Open doors and windows look less alarming if you stand farther away, although you may find that you don't have enough room to get back to a comfortable viewing distance. So cheat!

Follow the same steps as for the window on pages 24-25. Remember that each door has two vanishing points—one for the top, bottom and all the glazing bars, and one for the other edges as shown on page 25. To find the vanishing points for the open doors, draw a line parallel to the door drawn on the plan, from viewpoint up to picture plane and vertically down to eye-level. This locates the vanishing point for that edge of the door. Because the door has a thickness (which I hope you have described on your plan to scale) you will then draw a line parallel to that edge from the viewpoint to the picture plane and down to the eye-level. You will find that one vanishing point (the first) is quite close, and may be within the drawing itself, and that the other one is some distance away, outside the drawing. You may have to tape extra paper to the side of the drawing to locate its position.

Before you begin drawing the doors, take a moment to consider the opening, the hole in the wall where the doors and door frame exist. Everything can be drawn using exactly the same system as before. Take the back edge of the wall (in the plan) towards the viewpoint. Where this line crosses the picture plane, drop it down vertically and you will discover the position of the back edge of the wall in your projection on the elevation.

To find out what happens to the bottom and top edges of the opening, simply head towards a central vanishing point on the eye-level from the ground line and from the top of the opening, as it is in the real world, in other words, to scale. The point where you cross the vertical line that shows the back edge describes the depth of the wall in perspective. This works in the same way for the door frame, and having done this you will be ready for the door itself.

The vertical edges of the doors can be found using the same system (i.e., from viewpoint to relevant point in plan, across picture plane, then vertically downwards). Now you can use the vanishing points to draw the doors properly. If the doors look strange, your viewpoint is too close.

Practice this method by doing projections of straight-forward shapes and architectural features. You will soon master this. Once you have, you will be able to achieve convincing realism in your work.

To Summarize

1 Using sensible guesswork as a guide to size, lay out a plan using a suitable scale (ideally 1:10 or 1:20), positioning features as you want them to appear. Show clearly the picture plane and extend it out to the sides.

2 Underneath the plan draw an elevation to the same scale centered on the center of the plan showing the ground line, height of the wall and width of the opening and adding the eye-level which should also be extended out to the sides.

3 Position the viewpoint on the plan marking it clearly.

4 Connect the main points in the plan with the viewpoint and project them down vertically to find their new position in the elevation.

5 Locate the relevant vanishing points by drawing lines parallel to edges shown in the plan from the viewpoint up to the picture plane, and project vertically down to meet the eye-level.

6 Complete the elevation.

7 Measure the reference points on the drawing and convert them back to full-size to position the elements on the wall.

Common Perspective Problems

Using the vanishing point and the eye-level, it helps to imagine a column as square (Fig 1). Then use diagonals to divide the square as shown (Fig 2). A circle touches the four sides in the middle of each side and is much easier to position and draw like this. It gives the top and base of columns (or, for that matter, anything else with a circular top or base) a much more convincing shape.

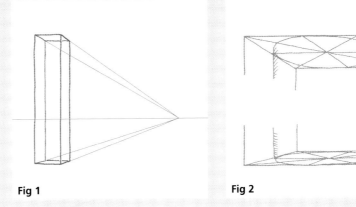

Fig 1

Fig 2

To find the perspective center of a square or rectangle (e.g., the side of a building), use the vanishing point, then the diagonals. The area can first be halved, then quartered, and so on (Fig 3).

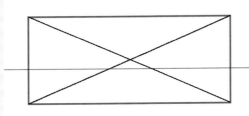

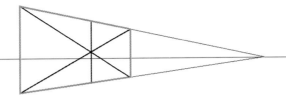

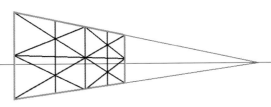

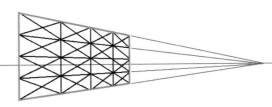

KEY
- Black lines: *elements in real life, including edges of painted "opening"*
- Red lines: *eye-level*
- Blue lines: *imaginary elements*
- Green lines: *important "construction" lines*

Fig 3

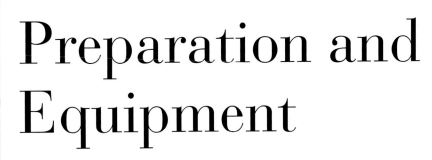

Preparation and Equipment

Like anything in life, things can be done "on the cheap" or you can spend as much money and time as you have available to achieve the desired result. I subscribe to the view that when tackling any project it's a good idea to assemble the tools you already have and then add a couple of new things. I always recommend buying good quality brushes and paints whenever possible (cheap brushes fall apart, losing hairs and shape). Use paints and brushes you feel comfortable with, i.e., ones that are easy to handle. Anything that intimidates you is best left alone (I often feel overwhelmed by very expensive brushes and end up not using them in case I spoil them).

Look at the surface on which you are going to paint and decide how best to prepare it. Traditionally the painting would be done directly on a wall, but it is also possible to paint on panels that can be "custom-made" and fitted to the chosen wall space.

Preparing surfaces to paint on is almost as important as doing the painting itself. This trompe l'oeil was painted on the walls surrounding a swimming pool so, because the surface would be constantly splashed, I used 100 percent acrylic paint. To add extra protection, the walls were varnished with clear 100 percent acrylic varnish.

Painting on Walls

Painting on the wall in the room we are planning to enhance is the favorite option. We will have the feel of the environment, the scale of it, its natural light qualities and an idea of the perspective which will be easy to "eyeball."

The surface may have been painted in the past. It may be rough, unstable, damp, flaking or pitted. The paint previously used may not be compatible with the materials we intend to use in our trompe l'oeil. All these things need to be considered before we begin.

When confronted with a situation that requires expert advice, talk to a good decorator or seek help from a DIY shop. Give them the facts about the wall, the kind of punishment the surface is going to take and your own painting preferences, and listen to what they recommend. Experts enjoy sharing their knowledge. They are the sort of people who make the world tick, the sort whose knowledge passes down through generations like the paintings themselves. When in doubt, find someone who knows! Don't feign knowledge; it will only land you in trouble.

In an ideal world we would ask for a fresh, newly plastered surface. The surface can be pink plaster (a color which I always think makes a wonderful base color for painting—see page 49), or a smooth cement surface. A plaster surface is smoother and, therefore, kinder to brushes. Inevitably, there will be less natural texture on the wall surface, which may be seen as an advantage or a disadvantage depending on your own individual preference. I love working on cement surface as it has a little more "bite" to it.

If working with a builder, ask him to produce a flat, even surface, completely free from damp. Really emphasize this point. A wall can be affected from behind as much as from the front, and in a way, modern paints are better suited to dealing with conditions that affect the surface we look at than with the disorders that can affect the condition of the wall itself. No one wants to spend time and effort on a painting that lifts from the wall after a short period. A wall exposed to the outside on the other side is also susceptible to damage from the elements unless properly sealed from the outside. Ask a builder for proper advice and don't be tempted to skip these stages.

A wall that has been plastered specially for mural painting must be allowed to dry. This means that plaster or cement surface should have time to let all water content evaporate. Nothing is more disheartening than spending several weeks working on what you believed to be a stable surface, and then having a crack appear from top to bottom through your painting. This is likely to happen with a new surface which has been artificially "cured" with the help of a dehumidifier or too much heat. Do not start until sufficient time has elapsed (perhaps several weeks) for the natural drying of the surface. Remember the drying time will be longer in winter than in summer. may be necessary to use a dehumidifier if time is of the essence.

Assuming that the wall has been correctly rendered and plastered, when you begin to paint, make sure that the air temperature in the room is high enough to allow the paint to set satisfactorily.

Preparing the surface

Unfortunately newly plastered walls are not always available to us, and we may have to make do with what we've got. Don't be put off! Beautiful effects can be achieved on the most irregular of surfaces. When confronted with a less-than-perfect surface, turn it to your advantage. Think of all the wonderful frescoes you have seen and admired. Think how marvelous an aged painting looks, with its faded or darkened colors peeling from the antique canvas. There's something mysterious and intriguing about it. Its history is shown in the nature of the deterioration, and that deterioration itself can be studied and exploited to help you to produce a fascinating mural. Incorporate the texture into your design and make the most of it.

It is important to stabilize a poor wall as much as possible, using products specially designed to seal and bond a surface, such as a water-based or acrylic sealer. As before, seek expert advice. Describe your surface in great detail and use the recommended products to prime the wall, making sure that conditions are suitable at the time for painting and priming.

If the wall has been previously painted, it's important to find out about prior applications. Limewashes must be removed, as overpainting a limewash does not work. This can be softened, and removed by a steam wallpaper-stripper. Painting in acrylic (water-based) paints on top of old oil paint also does not

work. Either strip the wall completely, or continue to use oil-based paint, or find out about products that can be used to isolate the oil from future applications of paint. You can use a polyvinyl acetate (PVA) or acrylic sealer here, painted on in thin layers.

Priming the wall

The wall needs to be primed with a suitable paint that will act as the base coat for the painting. Primers are either oil-based, in which case you want an alkali-resisting type, or water-based acrylic or non-acrylic. Because technology changes so fast, always ask the advice of an expert at the very outset.

Oil paints seal the surface of a wall, whereas acrylic paints allow the wall to breathe through the paint. Although I would not suggest that you paint onto a wall that is not completely dry, it must be considered that acrylic paints and emulsions will allow some flexibility if there is any doubt about the surface.

Diluting the first coat of paint is sometimes recommended by manufacturers, but be careful not to dilute the paint more than recommended, as this will affect the adhesion to the surface.

My favorite primer is gesso, now sold in ready-mixed acrylic form (you used to have to boil rabbit skin to make it!), but the cost of it on a large project is often prohibitive. Emulsion paint would be a suitable alternative.

Applying paint

When priming a wall in preparation for your mural, there are some basic rules for applying paint to achieve a good long-lasting surface.

Paints are either oil-based or water-based, but the two types don't mix. It is possible to cover a water-based paint with an oil paint, but not vice versa. In circumstances where a wall has been painted with oil and you really want to continue in acrylic, you must thoroughly sand the wall to improve the adhesion. (Make sure that you wear a face mask while doing this, as the dust from the old paint may be toxic). After sanding, use a suitable primer on the wall before starting work.

You can use the existing wall surface to your advantage, especially where you want the finished surface to look highly textured, as in this case. Where the wall has a rough surface, you must make sure that it is stable before you start painting, but the finished effect can benefit tremendously from the added texture.

On fresh plaster or a sand and cement surface on normal interior walls, a thin coat of emulsion diluted 3 parts paint to 1 part water will suffice as a priming coat, and as you will see on page 49, this does not need to be white but can be a color chosen to help with your painting.

Walls surrounding swimming pools or exterior walls can be primed using 100 percent acrylic sealer, which is totally impervious to water.

Painting on Panels

As mentioned earlier, it is possible to paint "off site" on made-to-measure panels that can then be fixed to the walls at a later date, assuming you have the appropriate studio facilities to do the painting elsewhere.

As with walls, there are advantages and disadvantages to doing this. Clearly, working away from the actual situation, you are not as familiar with the surroundings, and, therefore, must go to great lengths to be sure of eye-levels and light sources that may affect the painting if the aim is to achieve a certain degree of realism. This is particularly important in dealing with perspective, when the viewpoint must be clearly understood.

Transporting the panels can be a risky business, although with expert packing and careful delivery (there are firms who specialize in the carriage of items like these), there is no reason why this should cause a problem. The size of the work must be measured taking into account entrances, doorways, staircases and hairpin bends. You must be prepared to repair damage caused in transit.

There are various methods of affixing rigid panels to the existing walls. You can use "secret fixing" which is a little like the hook-and-eye system of fastening trousers. Countersunk screws can be used, the disadvantage being that some touching-up will be required to conceal the evidence. There are also very strong contact adhesives available. These are recommended only where permanence is assured.

The advantages of painting on panels may outweigh the disadvantages. You can move the painting in the future (providing that you didn't use the aforementioned contact adhesive, which is likely to pull the wall down as well!) and take it with you when you move house. You have a wonderfully stable surface on which to

This trompe l'oeil painting of The Monk was done on a large panel of MDF (see page 91 for more details).

work, one that can be beautifully prepared and primed, and, perhaps the most important of all, you don't need to be in anybody's way while you paint it! If the area to be painted is very large, you may be able to conceal joints in the panels cleverly in the design itself. Quite often a mural may be part of other ongoing home improvements, but an artist deep in thought can be a very irritating obstruction to electricians and plumbers going about their daily business!

There are several different surfaces suitable for custom-made murals. My own preference is for MDF (medium density fiberboard), as it is very stable, rigid and strong. It comes in several different thicknesses and sizes, and can easily be cut to the exact dimensions required, although if cutting it yourself, you must be careful not to inhale the dust produced during the cutting. The drawbacks of MDF should be considered. It is susceptible to damage from damp unless completely sealed, so prime it on the back as well as the front, so that it is completely protected. Painting the back helps to prevent warping. It can also be damaged by impact on the corners. There is a slight possibility that MDF may have a limited life, although this is not yet known for certain.

Other portable surfaces include canvas and architects' drafting film, which I personally don't enjoy much, as I find it too smooth. Canvas can be stretched as for normal painting, then cut to size and glued to the surface with contact adhesive (ask your art supplier how to do this). The trouble with canvas is that the larger the area, the more vulnerable it becomes to the damage in transit (it is usual to transport it rolled up). It also becomes rather awkward to stick on, since the larger it gets, the heavier and more limp it becomes. The canvas should be stuck on by an expert.

Priming MDF panels

MDF is best primed with two coats of acrylic gesso, rubbed down with fine sandpaper between coats. This gives a wonderfully absorbent surface and can be improved afterwards by staining whatever color you wish, although you can also buy gesso in a variety of colors.

When applying gesso, don't paint it on in neat square blocks; you can already use the background texture to your advantage in the development of texture and added drama in

Painting a Mural

Start by organizing yourself properly. Assemble your drawings and photographic references, out of the way of paint but always visible. Transparent plastic folders are a good form of protection. If you have found your references in expensive books, make good quality color photocopies. Spread your reference material out to one side.

Put down suitable floor protection in case of spills and tape it down around the edges, with an extra layer where you will be mixing paint. An old piece of hardboard or another table is good for mixing paint on. On the floor I use dust or polythene sheeting because it's waterproof. You can also use old bed sheets or curtains.

In this painting I projected the image on to the wall. The trouble with using an overhead projector on this scale is that your own composition may be lost and unexpected distortion can occur. If you do use a projector, it may be better to sketch out the subject freehand first in a faint color to decide the size and position of the image.

Using Colors

Lay out your colors so that they are conveniently displayed to you. It's very annoying to have to rummage for colors when you are concentrating on the painting. As you gain experience you will discover which are your favorite colors, but to begin with I suggest that you use the range shown below. Whatever the scale of your project, and whatever sort of paint you plan to use, you should be able to achieve a good range with these basic colors.

These are the names given to colors in some of the American and British paint ranges, but for a project where you are using say household emulsion paint, check the names of these colors on an acrylic paint index against an index showing the range you want to use.

Using the color index

Look carefully at references for color guidance, either something you can observe for real or a well-printed photograph. If you have in front of you some photos showing the mood that you are looking for, half-shut your eyes and see if you can tell whether there is background warmth in the shot. By this I mean whether warm colors are present, e.g., pinks, oranges, yellows, browns, because this will guide you towards a suitable color for the background. You don't need to use the same picture as the one from which your composition is drawn. Just find one which has the right kind of color (even if you used a particular photo during the designing of the composition of the mural you may be able to improve on the color by looking at another photo). If you stare at the picture for some time you will be amazed how you gradually become more conscious of the colors.

This is where the DIY color index comes in handy. The more colors there are in the index, the better. Simply "match" areas in the reference to selected parts of the photograph, and then make a note of your choice in pencil on the index or stick a note to it. The idea here is to mix up color exactly as it is shown in your reference. For a small project you can do this as you go, hoping that you can repeat it when required, but mixing larger quantities for a bigger painting and keeping the paint in airtight containers will be worth the time spent doing it.

You can do this as many times as you have the patience for, the principle being that the

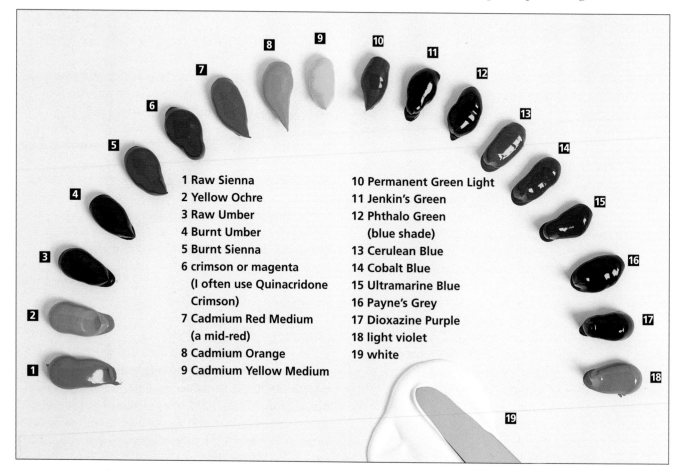

1 Raw Sienna
2 Yellow Ochre
3 Raw Umber
4 Burnt Umber
5 Burnt Sienna
6 crimson or magenta
   (I often use Quinacridone
   Crimson)
7 Cadmium Red Medium
   (a mid-red)
8 Cadmium Orange
9 Cadmium Yellow Medium
10 Permanent Green Light
11 Jenkin's Green
12 Phthalo Green
   (blue shade)
13 Cerulean Blue
14 Cobalt Blue
15 Ultramarine Blue
16 Payne's Grey
17 Dioxazine Purple
18 light violet
19 white

For a Foxglove Pink (as used on page 98), mix white, Cadmium Orange, Cadmium Red and Quinacridone Crimson.

For the light brown used for columns (see page 102), mix white, Yellow Ochre, Payne's Grey and Burnt Sienna.

For the green used for trees (see page 74), mix Cobalt Blue, Permanent Green Light, Yellow Ochre, Cadmium Red Medium, white, Raw Umber, Cadmium Yellow Medium and Payne's Grey.

For the shade of white used on a window frame (see page 94), mix white, Cobalt Blue, Cadmium Orange and Permanent Green Light.

greater the range, the more realism you will have in your painting. This will help to isolate the color and make it easy to identify. Start by picking out just a few obvious areas of color that are easy to see, like different parts of the sky. Complexity will develop with practice.

As an exercise, try observing colors in this way in real life. Ask yourself to solve questions like "what color is the road in front of me, both in the sun and in the shade?" You will be very surprised! What color is the grass just outside my window, and farther away into the distance? And what about the sky, just above the horizon and higher up? Try sorting out the different shades of a "white" window frame—the surface that faces you, and the edge that points inwards and catches the light. You will find that one side is probably a different color from the other, and by shutting one eye and holding the color index at a comfortable distance in front of you, you can flick through until you find exactly the same color. Make notes on the index in pencil so that you can erase later. If you haven't got an index, lay a piece of thin clear plastic on top of the image you are using and mix paint until a blob of it "disappears" into what you are looking at, in other words it's a perfect color match.

Make sure that the light on the color chart is similar to what you are looking at. It's no good trying to find the color of a lovely blue sky by looking at it from inside a room. You have to take yourself outside and allow the color index to be exposed to similar light conditions to that which you are looking at. This will help you to research all the colors you will need to begin your painting and really understand the way one color affects another.

In this way you will learn to find out about the color of objects and, believe me, you will be amazed how all your previous ideas will be swept aside and how a new awareness of color begins to grow.

All this may seem remarkably pedantic, but it's so much easier to paint when your palette contains the right ingredients. It's just like cooking. You can't produce cordon bleu cuisine unless you prepare the ingredients properly before you start! It really is worth the effort.

Mixing colors

Until you feel confident that you are mixing color along the right lines, try small quantities on a palette so that you don't waste paint. Lay out a blob about 1cm (½") long of each color that you have around the edge of the palette. It's always better to offer the complete range at your disposal so that you can get into the habit

Tuscan View

This painting was commissioned specifically to brighten up an ordinary kitchen wall, opening it out into a different time and place. During the long, wet winter months, the occupants of this house can gaze at a sunny Tuscan landscape, fondly remembering holidays spent there.

I used pictures from travel brochures to plan the landscape, sourcing ideas from about a dozen different places. The peacock is my own, and he tends to creep into a lot of my paintings. I find him hard to resist and he adds a certain exotic quality to the design. The owners were delighted when I suggested including their dog in the mural.

The Stone Floor

7 Using a fine sable brush and a mixture of Payne's Grey and Raw Umber, work the paint in to the "cracks" between the slabs, varying the thickness of the line as much as is possible.

8 When the paint has dried, use a small piece of medium sandpaper to rub gently over the work. This helps to exaggerate the texture and bring it to life. Don't rub too hard or you will remove the layers of paint and expose the surface behind.

9 Don't worry if the sandpaper removes some of the lines. Simply paint them in again with deeper colors, such as Jenkins Green mixed with Dioxazine Purple, improving the detail of the painting all the time. Don't expect to achieve a perfect result immediately—just continue building the paint up in layers, making each stone slab a slightly different color from its neighbor.

The Balustrade

STEP-BY-STEP

It's always best to make a stencil for this kind of repetitive shape as it means you can continually reproduce the original shape of the stone pillars correctly and with the right spacing between them. The card stencil can then be kept for any future paintings requiring a similar balustrade.

Paint	Equipment
Raw Umber	Tracing paper
Payne's Grey	Soft and hard pencils
White	Ruler
Yellow Ochre	Craft knife and cutting board
Burnt Sienna	Stencil paper (this can be made by priming cartridge paper on both sides with emulsion paint, but the bought paper is better)
Jenkins Green	
Permanent Green Light	
Dioxazine Purple	
Ultramarine Blue	
Cadmium Red	
	Masking tape
	Natural sponges
	1cm (½") flat brush
	Fine pointed brush
	Fine sandpaper

1 Tape a sheet of tracing paper over the sketched balustrade. Make a rough tracing from your full-size freehand sketch to establish the right size and general shape of the balustrade. Make sure the curves at the base look right for the eye-level—"eyeball" this!

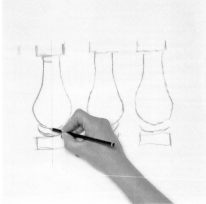

2 To refine this tracing, trace over again one half of the curve and mark the center by ruling a faint line. Fold the tracing paper down the center line and trace over the half-outline to make a complete pillar.

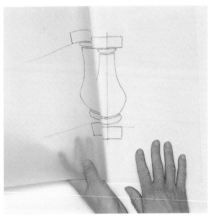

3 Fold the tracing paper down a center line between the position of two pillars and trace over the first drawing to repeat the first shape exactly.

The Dog

STEP-BY-STEP

When planning this part of the trompe l'oeil I used my camera as a design tool, looking down on the small dog in real life as I would in the finished painting. When taking reference photographs of the dog, I positioned her and the camera carefully to make sure that the eye-level was correct. I wanted her to appear as if she was looking out into the garden. I also made sure that the "sunny side" of the animal was the correct side, i.e., the right, so that I could paint in shadows accurately.

Paint

Full palette of colors (see page 46)

Equipment

Fine pointed brush

8mm (⅜") flat brush

1 Using your reference, start by sketching an outline using the fine pointed brush, with a color only slightly darker from the background color but still visible. You can do this freehand, using an overhead projector or by squaring it up (see page 50).

2 Loosely paint the dog using a full palette of colors and an 8mm (⅜") flat brush. Start to describe areas of light and shade and add a few vague details. For the lighter areas of her coat I used Payne's Grey, white and Yellow Ochre; the dark patches were Payne's Grey, Raw Umber and white.

3 Remember that the white French doors are the most important aspect of the mural and to allow them to dazzle above all else, we must not get too bright anywhere else, so add a hint of Payne's Grey and Yellow Ochre to the "white" bits of the dog. She will still appear white. Use the smaller brush to paint detail and continue building up the roundness of the dog, working from light to shade and back again.

The Tuscan Village

STEP-BY-STEP

I found a suitable picture of a village on a hill in a travel brochure. You could make an acetate from your reference photograph and project the village if you are doubtful about the composition of it. The great thing about scribbling on acetate is that you can do it as often as you like until it fits where you want it to!

Paint

Full palette of colors
(see page 46)

Equipment

Fine pointed brush

8mm (⅜") flat brush

Toothbrush

1 Working from reference, begin with a very loose faint outline, roughly defining a few roof shapes and not worrying about any detail at this stage. This is just to help you decide on the actual position of the village in the landscape.

2 Using a full palette of colors and the 8mm (⅜") flat brush, start to block in the main areas (for sky see page 109). Keeping the sky much darker and duller than you would imagine will make the buildings gleam in the sun. You can use the color index to choose your main colors (see page 46).

3 Keep redefining areas of sun and shade with the angle of the sun fixed in your mind as you paint. This will help to make the buildings three-dimensional even though the shapes are simple. The same applies to the surrounding trees and bushes which fill in the spaces. Use the 8mm (⅜") flat brush for all this painting.

4 Work deeper into the shadowy areas, mixing Payne's Grey and Ultramarine Blue into the colors. Think hot and cool colors—sun and shade—and keep working from one to the other. There is not much detail in this but it's surprising how a simple idea can be developed in this way.

5 Using a toothbrush, flick some of the sky color over the hillside and village to soften the outlines.

Tabby Cat

Why paint a trompe l'oeil cat as if it was staring down into the bath looking for fish to catch? The answer is very simple—purely for fun! This is one of those small visual jokes that I refer to in the Introduction on page 6—it is just meant to amuse the onlooker. I was flattered to find that not only the humans in our house were interested in the cat; all the dogs had a good look at it as well before deciding that it didn't smell quite right and failed to move.

I photographed this cat with the idea for the trompe l'oeil already clear in my mind, so I ensured I captured him at the right angle and used the resulting photos as the basis for my painting. The painting itself was completed in one session. When working quickly like this, it is essential to ensure that each paint application is dry before progressing to the next stage so that there is no danger of the previously painted layer coming away. Extending the tail on to the timber bath edge emphasizes the three-dimensional effect. A painting of this size is ideal for a beginner, as good results can be achieved in a short period.

Guinea Fowl

These guinea fowl have been painted sitting on top of the door frame and at other strategic points around the room. The point of painting them in unexpected places is the element of surprise and humor! It only works if you achieve a life-like quality with a clean outline.

Not very many people keep these birds, so I was lucky to have these subjects in my own garden to observe. However, in order to see what they looked like from below, I did have to get up extremely early to take reference photographs of them before they descended from their normal perch in the oak tree. The reason for this is a matter of perspective. The eye-level of the observer would naturally be lower than the birds, so to make them look realistic, I needed to view them from a similar angle.

Small Projects

Paints	Equipment
Payne's Grey	Tracing paper
White	Soft and hard pencils
Raw Umber	
Burnt Sienna	Fine pointed brush
Quinacridone Crimson	1cm (½") and 2cm (¾") flat brushes
Ultramarine Blue	
Cadmium Red	
Cadmium Yellow	

The important thing about doing something like this bird, or the tabby cat featured on page 64, is that the wit of the joke will only be successful if you apply everything else in the book. By this I mean that considering the eye-level, doing the drawing well and matching colors to achieve realism will all contribute to the enjoyment of the onlooker. Keep the outline clean and well-defined.

A simple trompe l'oeil like this can have just as much impact in your house as a full-scale project but will only take a fraction of the time.

1 I took my outline from photographs of the guinea fowl. To enlarge the outline to the correct size, I squared it up (see page 50) onto a large piece of tracing paper. Draw with a soft pencil on the reverse side of the paper, then hold the paper against the wall and go over the outline again with a harder pencil on the right side to make a faint outline. Sketch in the outline using dilute Payne's Grey and white and a fine pointed brush.

2 Block in the solid bird shape with the 1cm (½") flat brush, using Payne's Grey, white, Raw Umber and Burnt Sienna with more Payne's Grey in the shadowy areas. Continue with the same four colors, working deeper into the shadow areas to describe the shape of the bird. Bear in mind the direction of the light.

3 Add a little Quinacridone Crimson, and Ultramarine Blue to the shadow side of the neck using a 1cm (½") flat brush. At this stage, the painting is quite sketchy. It is important to wait for each application of paint to dry before beginning the next color, otherwise it will slide off the wall when you overpaint.

4 Rough in the red parts of the head with Cadmium Red using a small pointed brush. Add the eye, nostril, horn and legs, using Burnt Sienna, Cadmium Red and Cadmium Yellow. Also put in the shadows and folds of the red parts with crimson, Burnt Sienna and Payne's Grey. The head is pure white and should stand out against the off-white background.

5 Add highlights and shadows to the chest area using a 1cm (½") flat brush, working more into the shadows and always softening between highlight and shadow as you work over the previous coat. It helps to imagine the bird without its spots.

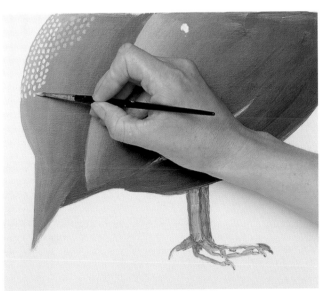

6 Now you are ready to do the spots. Look closely at your reference or first sketch the pattern of the spots on paper to look at. Don't worry too much about accuracy—no one really counts spots on guinea fowl! Using a fine pointed brush, paint patches of spots and then fill in the gaps. Make the spot shape elliptical near the edges to add to the illusion of roundness. Use white in the sunlit areas, and grey (by adding Payne's Grey) in the shadows in varying amounts depending on the darkness.

7 Using a 2cm (¾") flat brush and the background color, tidy up the edges of the guinea fowl for a neat finish.

Cattle Murals

These paintings were commissioned by David Bennett who wanted to commit his favorite cow and bull to posterity. The bull is led by his herdsman, dressed in nineteenth-century clothing which he felt suitable for the occasion.

The bull and cow were long since deceased but David had pictures of them from which I could establish their markings. I painted the cow standing in front of Blair Castle in Scotland as that was where she had gone to live when David had sold her. For reference I used a photo of the castle.

Painting Trees

STEP-BY-STEP

Paints

Cadmium Red

Yellow Ochre

Cadmium Yellow

Permanent Light Green

Cobalt Blue

Payne's Grey

Raw Umber

White

Equipment

5mm (¼") flat brush

1cm (½") flat brush

Fine pointed brush

The tree in this painting is a rather stylised elm. It was painted on a tinted surface (see page 49). The redness helps foliage look more lively. First work out what sort of tree you want in your painting as every tree is different. The best way to learn about tree colors is to take the color index (see page 46) outside and look at trees, trying to match selected patches of color to a particular card. This will teach you that tree greens, like grass greens, are amazingly red, and you will need to add surprising amounts of Cadmium Red to each color. To paint a tree like this you need seven colors: four greens, and three trunk colors, i.e., a sort of greeny-grey in three tones.

If you are working on a big scale, it may help to paint the leaves with a sponge roller cut into leaf patterns with a craft knife. You could also make a leaf stencil. Leaves on a tree tell you what sort of tree it is, and all the leaves are exactly the same size and shape, but viewed from slightly different angles, so that a stencil with, say, five leaves at different angles to the viewpoint could be used to paint huge areas of foliage. This tree, however, is small and fairly simple.

The rough edges are intentional, as if the new paint has been scraped off to reveal these paintings underneath.

1 First, block in the approximate shape of the foliage with the second darkest green, using a 1cm (½") flat brush. This actually shows the reverse side of the tree, where the leaves face outwards—you are looking at the backs of these leaves.

2 Using a mixture of Raw Umber and Payne's Grey and a fine pointed brush, sketch in the skeleton of the tree. Remember that a tree must be well balanced; otherwise it will fall over! This is best learned by observation.

3 Next, visualize branches coming towards and going away from you. With the pointed brush, pick out some of the tops of the branches (remembering the direction of the light source) in a lighter color, e.g., Raw Umber, Payne's Grey, white and a little Yellow Ochre.

4 Instead of picturing all the individual leaves and twigs on the tree, simplify the leaves into clumps of foliage and imagine them pointing towards you and sideways. Paint them with a 1cm (½") flat brush and the lightest green for the topsides, the middle shade for the bulk of the clump, and the darkest shade for the shadowy undersides.

5 Carry on painting in this way, building up convincing clumps of foliage. I used a 5mm (¼") flat brush and a fine sable for the small branches. Don't be afraid to rework the branches in gaps between the leaves.

6 Finally, bring the sky and background colors in to outline the tree, and using a 5mm (¼") brush, puncture the green canopy with dots of the sky colors to make the whole tree look less solid.

En Grisaille

En Grisaille implies that little or no color has been used in the painting, giving it a monochromatic effect. This project wouldn't appeal to those with insufficient patience, as the technique I used here to produce this rather ghostly effect is time-consuming but very satisfying when finished. My clients had enormous fun choosing the nine characters featured on the walls. The room ended up being quite extraordinary.

En Grisaille Details

The walls of this room were very uneven, so to disguise this I used a highly textured background and a splattered effect for the painting. The balustrade was the first element of the work, concealing a bump which circled the entire room where a dado rail had been removed. Once the balustrade existed there seemed to be an amazing space outside it, as though the actual surface of the walls had disappeared. This was when the mythological figures came into being, one by one, until there were nine in total, including Pegasus, the winged horse; Neptune, god of the sea; and Athena, goddess of war, wisdom and the arts and crafts.

All the figures are mythological, except for the man climbing over the trompe l'oeil balustrade, who appears to be intruding into this fantasy. He was the first to be painted and was dressed in clothes copied from late-eighteenth century Piranesi prints. Climbing into the room, his eyes are fixed on his lover who is dressed as Athena. Perhaps they are both aware of the other fantastic figures. She holds up a golden bridle, inviting him to jump on to the back of Pegasus. The other seven figures gaze at this from their ghostly world outside the balustrade. Only the man and woman are "real" which is why they are painted in color (see pages 80-81).

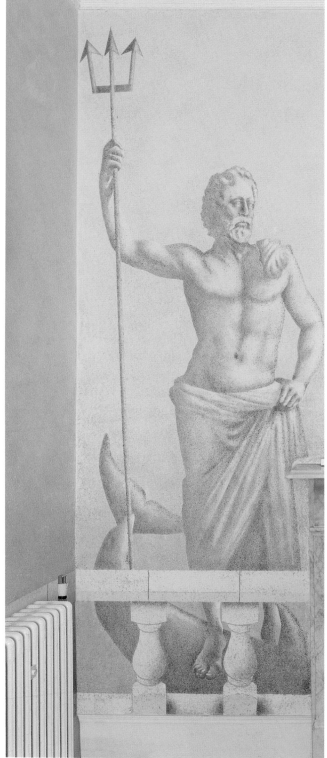

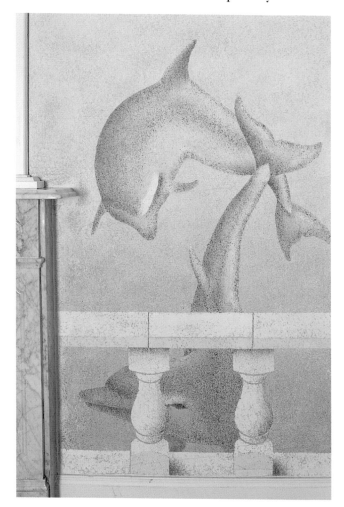

Changing Room

The funny thing about the keys and the banknote in this trompe l'oeil is that they are what people notice. The curtains which "dress" the arch through to the swimming pool, and all the fictitious clothing hanging on the pegs to the right, even the lady's bottom sticking out from behind the billowing curtain often escape the attention of the onlooker, but never the money and the keys!

My brief was to decorate the long wall by the indoor pool at the Nare Hotel in Cornwall, England. There was no point trying to surpass the stunning views—the scenery is far too beautiful to compete with. So I did the opposite, painting something very down-to-earth but "tongue in cheek."

Fabric Effects

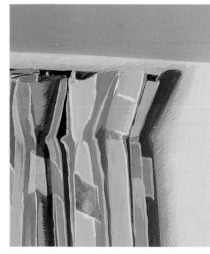

Above Making fabric look as though it is scrunched up can be done (in this case) by making the stripes on the material much narrower where the curtain tape would be, and also changing to "shadow" colors in the "cracks."

Right Humor is an important factor in trompe l'oeil. Did she know that her bottom was sticking out? In order to learn how to paint any part of the human anatomy, find out about local life painting classes. As usual, my best advice is that observation can solve all the problems you may think you have! All the information you need is right in front of you if you choose to look!

The whole room was repainted at my request, so that I would not have to work on a white background. White walls are an absolute killer for trompe l'oeil effects, as there is no "room" for painting highlights. You need to save white for special occasions to gain the maximum impact of its brightness. The background color that I often use in a situation like this where the client would prefer the room to look white is 0705Y10R. This color is a very subtle pale creamy-greeny-grey. It's much nicer than white anyway!

These clothes were all painted from life. To help me to look carefully at the folds of the fabric, I hung and draped the clothes around me, making sure the light was always on the left so they appeared to be lit by light from the window of the pool. The idea was that the swimmers had left their clothes hanging on the pegs, revealing a little of their characters!

The Monk

My research for this painting took me to Buckland Abbey. I photographed a model of the abbey and its surrounding buildings to help the composition of the "outside." The background landscape was sheer fantasy, based on a mixture of inspiration from the front cover of a magazine and our local Camel Estuary, looking out towards Padstow. I painted this monk on a panel for a trompe l'oeil exhibition in London, but I had in mind a particular spot in a wonderful priory in Somerset, which was being renovated. He is a Cistercian monk, gazing down into the cloister from high above, lost in thought, and oblivious to the dove, who has not noticed the cat, who has not noticed the mouse.

If you tip the picture plane forwards (as if tipping a sheet of glass) in order to look down (see page 18), the horizon naturally rises, which is why the distant hills are higher than the normal 1.5m (5') eye level. I used all sorts of tricks to make the outside much lighter and brighter than the gloomy interior where he stands. The whole painting started with a vigorous sponging and washing of warm diluted colors, mixtures of Cadmium Red, Burnt Sienna, Yellow Ochre and Cadmium Yellow with a good bit of flicking with toothbrushes and dabbing with dishcloths. By overpainting the "interior" bits with washes of Payne's Grey and Raw Umber, I was quickly able to establish the feeling of being in a gloomy place looking out into the bright daylight.

Monk's Sleeve

In this area of the trompe l'oeil I wanted to make the cloth of the monk's habit look colorless and murky, so I draped some similar lengths of fabric to see how colors were affected as they lost light in the depths of the folds. Glazing over, as expained in step 5, helped to keep the monk in his gloom.

Paints	Equipment
Payne's Grey	1cm (½") flat brush
White	Fine pointed brush
Raw Umber	2.5cm (1") flat brush
Yellow Ochre	
Matte acrylic medium	

1 Using the 1cm (½") brush, sketch with diluted Payne's Grey and white onto the warm background and, even at this early stage, show the shadows by sketching with the brush. This helps you to work out the folds.

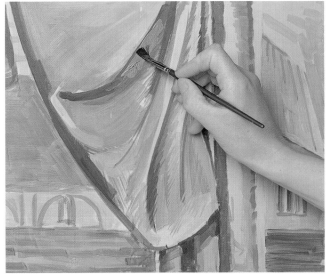

2 Block in the main areas very roughly, strengthening and extending the depth of the shadows with a mixture of Raw Umber and Payne's Grey. The main thing at this stage is to build up all areas of the painting loosely before starting to bring it together in any detail.

3 The lighter tones of the cloth can be shown in loose sweeping brush strokes, using the 1cm (½") brush and adding white and Yellow Ochre to the mixture of Payne's Grey and Raw Umber. Balance the darkness inside the building with the contrasting light outside (i.e., keep the figure darker than the landscape outside). Soften the folds by cross-hatching with color as you would with a pencil.

4 Using the same colors, keep building light and shade in and out of the folds of the fabric, softening all the time by cross-hatching. Some of the folds may need a fine brush. It really helps to have suitable fabric hanging close to you to look at, so that you know what it is you are trying to achieve. You can even use the color index (see page 46) to find colors in the folds of the fabric which will help so much to describe the texture.

5 To strengthen the darkness of the monk's habit use a dark glaze made with Raw Umber, Payne's Grey, and matte acrylic medium, applied with the 2.5cm (1") brush. Do this several times as it adds to the gloom, thereby exaggerating the brightness of the outside.

A Cornish Window

All murals have a reason, and here is the reason for this one! I don't need to have rural views painted inside my Cornish farmhouse, as all the views from the windows are wonderful. But for several years now we have had terrible weather during the summer, and the days when we can visit our favorite beach on the north coast are few and far between.

This year there was suddenly such a day. A crystal-clear, beautiful, shining day. The first glimpse of this beach as I clambered down the cliff path was so breathtaking that I felt moved to have this view out of a trompe l'oeil window behind the kitchen sink where my spirits most often need lifting. I had taken my camera and the color index with me and spent time considering the best view. I decided to balance the cliffs on the left by putting the open window on the other side.

Window Details

The flowers were a spontaneous addition. When I picked them, I had no idea that they would be so powerful. I just love wild flowers, and had no reservations about looking at them from the kitchen sink position, or from anywhere else in the room.

It is my belief that there is a kind of inner spiritual peace to be found during the painting of flowers from life. Avoid photographic reference wherever possible and look at the real thing. I find myself becoming inwardly calm and almost completely absorbed in the wonderful intricacies of petal colors and formations and thus entering a state of quiet, rather like the peace of a church or museum. There is something so amazing about the way a flower is put together that you can't help but be respectful and feel rather humble. The problem is to pack in enough observation and painting time before the flower fades in front of you.

Try to set aside enough time for this rather than do the painting over an extended period. The flowers will be long gone, but your impression of them will remain fresh forever. These flowers were all picked from the hedgerow and I had to replace some of them because as the painting progressed I couldn't work fast enough to capture the quality I was looking for.

There are full instructions for painting the sea and waves in The White Horses project on pages 105-108.

The Flowers

STEP-BY-STEP

This wall had one or two cracks and, having removed paintings from the wall and extracted the picture hooks, I needed to do some filling. I lightly sanded the whole wall and wiped it with a damp cloth before starting. I primed the area involved in the actual painting of the window with two coats of gesso, sanded between coats.

I used the color index (see page 46) to decipher colors, looking carefully at the sky, sea and sand, and making pencil notes on the color index. I had a lot of fun painting the sea, trying to make it transparent. The success of this depends on observation and using the right colors.

To paint the flowers, first draw in chalk on the background which may already be well advanced. Don't worry about finishing it before starting the flowers. It is almost impossible to paint so perfectly that you don't mark the bits you have already painted. It is better to try to amalgamate the two as you go, even if it means carefully painting around stalks and so on.

I used the projection method (see page 24) to establish the vanishing point for the top, bottom and glazing bars of the imaginary window.

The White Horses

I was amazed when a major beer company ran an advertising campaign just like this mural, and would have been fascinated to meet the designer who must have had identical thoughts on the subject, i.e., turning the crests of breaking waves into white horses leaping wildly from the water.

I adapted a Roman mosaic to form the basis of my design, and Neptune became a muscular surfer as this area of Cornwall is so famous for its surfers. The trompe l'oeil illusion was created by using a series of columns and arches along the length of the walls. Fragments of scattered masonry along the base of the wall help to suggest a collapsing ruin being reclaimed by the sea (not at all the case here at the Watergate Bay Hotel which has the most incredible views of the sea).

Sandstone Columns

When designing this trompe l'oeil I used a height of 1.5m (5') from the floor as my eye-level. This height therefore became the level for the horizon of the sea.

When you draw columns, start by imagining that they are square, not circular (see page 27). Using a vanishing point on the eye-level, you can draw the sides of the square to the vanishing point and then use the diagonals of the square base and top to draw a convincing circle in the correct perspective. Columns are narrower at the top and widen out roughly two-thirds of the way down. From there downwards, they are straight and true verticals.

Paints	Equipment
White	Chalk line
Payne's Grey	Radiator roller
Yellow Ochre	Car-washing
Burnt Sienna	sponge
Raw Umber	Fine sable brush
(For sky colors, see page 109)	

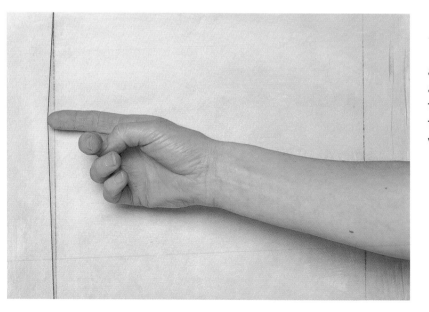

1 Mark out the columns using a chalk line, adding 1cm (½") to the width two-thirds of the way down.

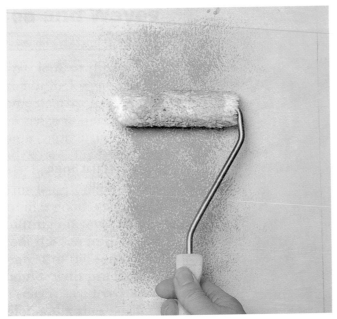

2 I used a radiator roller and three different sandstone colors—light, medium and dark, mixed as follows:

Light color: white, Payne's Grey, Yellow Ochre and Burnt Sienna

Medium color: white, Yellow Ochre and Burnt Sienna

Dark color: white, Raw Umber and Yellow Ochre.

Paint the middle of the column with the medium color.

3 The darkest bit is inside and off-center away from the strongest implied light source (i.e., from the left). Carry on using the three colors to form the cylinder using your imagination to feel the light (here, coming from the left, so the lightest color appears on the left).

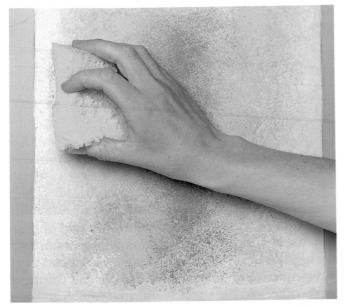

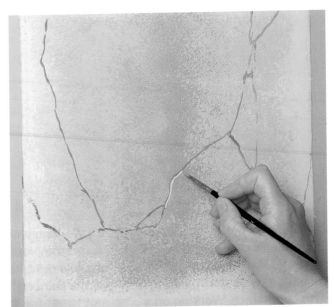

4 Painting the background in as soon as possible gives you something to relate to and make sure it's working. You can dab on the edge colors with a square-edged sponge. Develop the texture all over by repeatedly overpainting with sponges and rollers, using all three colors.

5 Finally, use a fine sable brush to add a few cracks, with a mixture of Raw Umber and Payne's Grey. It doesn't really matter how you do this, but remember to try and make them curve around the column. Highlighting the lower edge of the crack with a light color gives it more depth.

Painting Furniture

Trompe l'oeil can so easily be used on furniture to add both interest and, as usual, humor to an otherwise rather dull household object.

This is a decorative idea that might liven up any plain furniture. I wanted to make the wood really glow like mahogany. For the draped silk cloth I found a wonderful painting by Ingrès called *La Grande Odalisque*, which inspired this painting. It would have been acceptable, I think, to have just done the firescreen as if it was carved mahogany, but I liked the idea of the casually draped piece of silk damask. It begged the question who had left it there and why. An element of mystery always adds to trompe l'oeil!

The Firescreen

STEP-BY-STEP

Fireplaces can look very dingy in the summer when the fire's not lit, so why not add something a little exotic to a simple firescreen which can be purchased unpainted. I found a picture in a magazine of a Rococo carved mahogany bedhead which gave me the idea for the pattern at the top. I placed a polished mahogany chest near me in the studio so that I could observe what happened to its color both in the light and in shadow. To see how the damask worked I hung up my daughter's silk blouse to help me understand the folds in the fabric.

I first primed the screen with black gesso, then used two shades of reddish-brown glaze to make the surface gleam like wood. I used the color index (see page 46) to match the color to real mahogany. The paint was mixed with matte acrylic glaze to dilute it and make it more transparent.

Paints
Cadmium Red
Burnt Umber
Raw Umber
Dioxazine Purple
Ultramarine Blue
Jenkins Green
White
Payne's Grey
Light Violet
Yellow Ochre
Cadmium Yellow
Matte acrylic glaze (satin finish)

Equipment
Large hog's bristle domed continental brush
Tracing paper
2B and 6B pencils
Low-tack masking tape
8mm (⅜") flat brush
Fine pointed brush

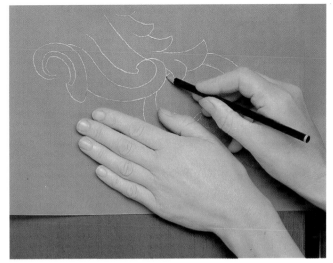

1 The glaze is made with Cadmium Red, Burnt Umber, Raw Umber and Dioxazine Purple, mixed with matte acrylic glaze. Paint it on with a large domed continental brush to leave streaks of the black showing through. Even after one coat, it's surprising how effective it is! Keep the brush strokes going in the same direction to create the woodgrain effect.

2 For the Rococo carving at the top, I found a magazine photograph of a carved mahogany bedhead. I adapted this to fit the firescreen and made a full-size drawing on tracing paper. You only need to do one side, as the other side (which is partly covered by the cloth) is just a mirror image of the same tracing. Draw on the reverse side of the tracing paper with a very soft 6B pencil, then tape the tracing to the screen and draw the design on the right side with a harder pencil. This will leave a pencil line on the firescreen for guidance.

3 Roughly paint in the draped silk cloth using the 8mm (³⁄₈") flat brush. I made four shades of the color of the cloth using Ultramarine Blue, Jenkins Green, white and Dioxazine Purple. Now using a mixture of Burnt Umber, Payne's Grey and Dioxazine Purple, sketch outside your pencil pattern guidelines to show the shadows cast by the wood carving. Don't worry if it's a bit sketchy—you can elaborate as you go.

4 Painting something to look three-dimensional is an exercise in light and shade. It is vital to be aware of the light source all the time, so paint deeper into the shadows and exaggerate the highlights (I used Light Violet and white for the highlights). I kept using my first mahogany colors to make the prominent carved shapes stand out from the shadows, highlighting them with the fine pointed brush and varying shades of Light Violet and white.

5 The draped damask could have been any fabric but I chose this extravagant fabric because I wanted something luxurious. It was painted entirely using four blue colors and the detailed embroidery shades of white, Yellow Ochre, Jenkins Green, Cadmium Yellow and Cadmium Red, which mixed together in different amounts make wonderful gold colors. I used the fine pointed brush to make the cross-hatching effect.

Tiepolo Mural

Some murals are not true trompe l'oeil, but could still be described as an "intent to deceive" as they mislead the onlooker into believing they are something which they are not. Sometimes a painting can be an admiration of the original artist's work, without any pretence that it's the real thing as the composition is different in order to fit available space. In this case, my client and I were fascinated by Tiepolo (1696-1770), so I painted several panels based on the work he did to decorate the Villa Valmarana. I had to alter the original compositions to fit the spaces available and in doing so I may have changed other things which were relevant to their original environment. It was a real pleasure painting these and discovering the various techniques Tiepolo used. You can learn so much from scrutinizing a famous artist's work.

Painting the Fan

STEP-BY-STEP

In the original painting, the fan was not patterned, but my client and I felt that Tiepolo might not mind this small alteration as my painting benefitted from the extra interest. Adding detail to an area of the painting can draw attention to that spot and can be quick to paint. The fun was making these murals look as if they were painted 250 years ago by "aging" the look of the painting!

Paints

Full palette of colors
(see page 46)

Equipment

8mm (⅜") flat brush

Dishcloth

Toothbrush

1 First, I sketched in the detail of the fan, working on one side at a time, then added white highlights.

2 Softening a complicated section of painting with an old dishcloth can add a vintage feel to the work in the simplest way. Fold the cloth into a pad and gently "blot" the paint before it dries.

3 Using an old toothbrush, flick paint of a contrasting color on to the painting to further age it, and help the brush strokes to disappear.

The Arches

Although my client had originally asked me to paint a mural with a "view" to the outside, I felt confident that an inner space would work better, especially as there were already French windows opening on to the garden from this lower ground floor room. Sometimes when a room already has a good view, I don't think there is any need to compete. It's better to use a bit of lateral thinking and approach the project from a different angle.

My first sketch showed how much "view" I wanted to see through the opening within the nearest arch. This is extremely important because part of the perspective drawing process in this case is affected by the position of the viewpoint (see page 16) which you need to ascertain. All the perspective was done using the projection method and this is a very useful exercise in precision.

The composition of the painting was loosely based on a magazine photograph of the library at Longleat House. It had a second, deeper arch beyond the first, through which you could see an ascending staircase and a window in the distance. The floor was to be the main challenge, as I intended to make it look as though it was an extension of the existing floor, for which I needed to work out the vanishing points for the floor tiles which were set at an angle of 45° to the picture plane (i.e., the wall).

Drawing the Plan

Step 3

Now the three vanishing points can be used to complete the perspective drawing (elevation). The central one will establish the correct position for all lines which are parallel to the direction of view, e.g., the tops and bottoms of the arches.

The two points out to the side on the eye-level, which were arrived at in Step 2, can be used to draw the floor tiles as shown, by connecting them to marks made where the tiles are full-size on the ground line. As you can see, in order to do the whole floor, you need to use imaginary marks further out to the sides along the ground line.

KEY
- Black lines: *elements in real life, including edges of painted "opening"*
- Red lines: *eye-level*
- Blue lines: *imaginary elements*
- Green lines: *important "construction" lines*

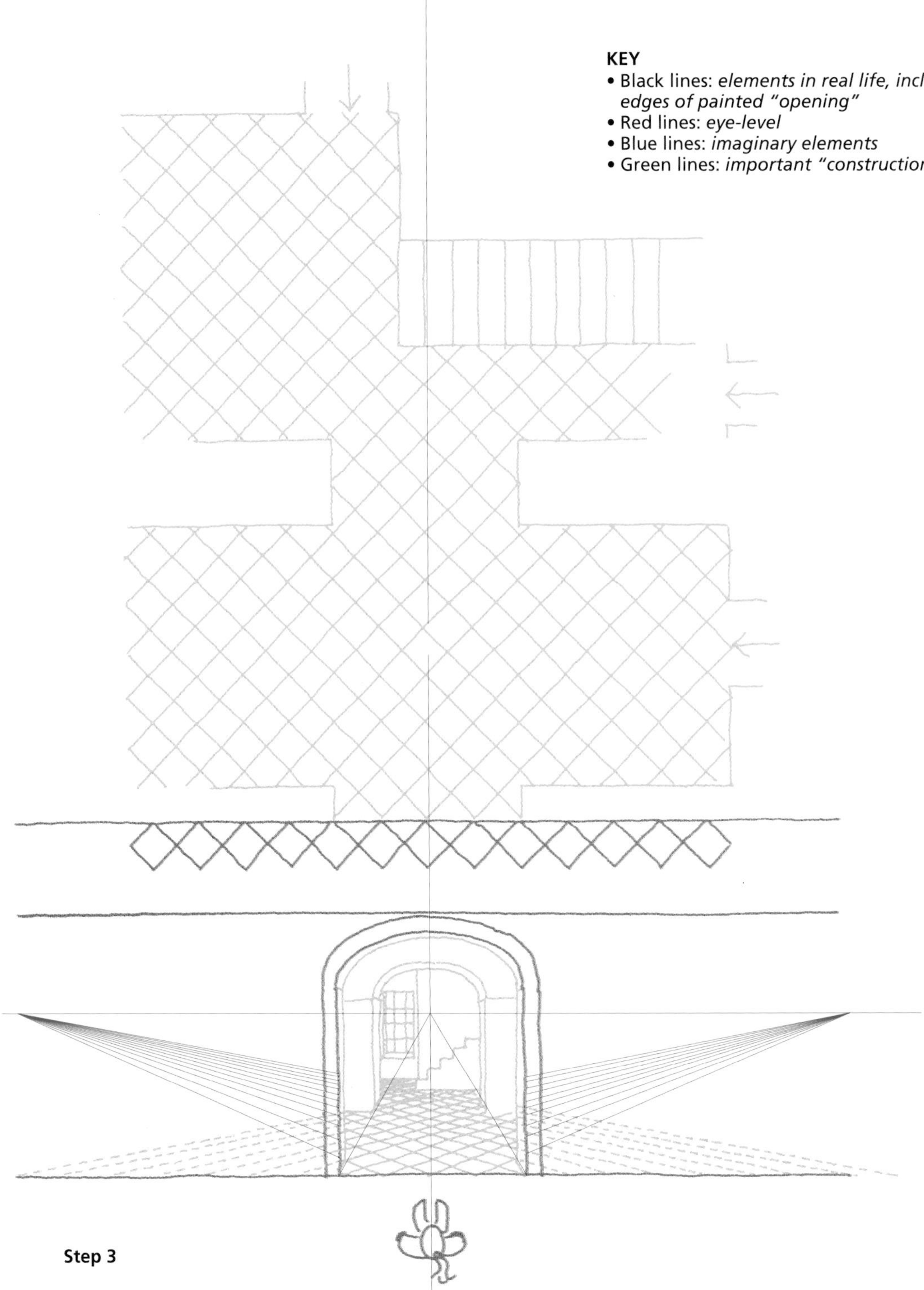

Step 3

Step 4

Mark out the outline of the stairs to scale on the elevation. Note the angle at which the staircase rises. Draw lines from the intersections of treads and risers back to the central vanishing point.

Returning to your plan, find the position of the staircase in your painting by establishing important points as before. Start with the bottom step and once drawn, the rest will follow. The staircase in your "view" will follow the same angle and each step will have the same dimensions as the first. Stairs rise at a constant angle, usually 35-40°.

Step 4

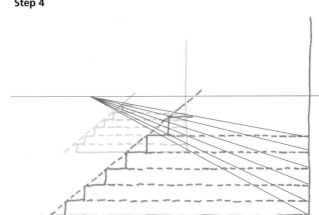

The Floor

To get the information from the drawing on to the wall, use reference points measured from the scale drawing and convert to full size, or trace the drawing on to acetate and project it, noting that the projector can distort architecture badly unless you are meticulous when positioning the projector, the wall is flat and vertical and the floor is level! The first method is more reliable.

The perspective shown here will only be totally convincing from one central viewpoint. If you were to step sideways it would no longer be completely accurate. Doing this could seem like a nightmare if you didn't have a few tricks up your sleeve! The idea of making a floor, tiled with square tiles set at 45° to the picture plane (i.e., wall), appear to continue in your mural is best achieved on site as a certain amount of "eyeballing" is called for. Most of the pain can be removed by technical preparation.

By glazing with thin paint (either mixed with water, or with matte acrylic medium or a retarding medium) you can achieve a chalky look which is especially good for natural stone floors.

Paints	Equipment
Raw Sienna	Masking tape
White	Scrap paper
Permanent Light Violet	Chalk line
Raw Umber	2.5cm (1") flat brush
Yellow Ochre	Natural sponge
Payne's Grey	8mm (⅜") flat brush
Matte acrylic medium or a retarding medium	Dishcloth
	Fine pointed brush

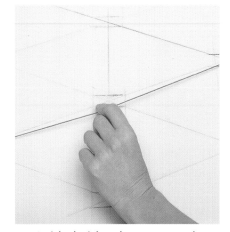

1 Guided either by measured reference points taken from your scale drawing or lines drawn with the overhead projector, use the chalk line to mark out the floor tiles. (An assistant is useful on a large mural). If you make a mistake, wipe off the chalk and do it again. Accuracy is very important and can be checked by making sure that the intersections between the tiles form a line to the central vanishing point.

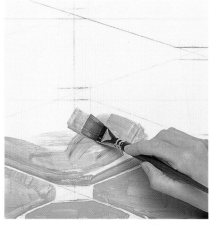

2 Using the 2.5cm (1") flat brush, start to block in the tiles, mixing different variations of the same color for each tile. Leave a tiny gap either side of the chalk line, but keeping close to it and straight. I matched the color of the existing tiles using Raw Sienna, white, Light Violet (a surprisingly good stone color when mixed with Yellow Ochre or Raw Sienna), and adding some Raw Umber where I wanted the tiles to look darker.

3 Carry on painting glazes using more Light Violet and white mixed with some Yellow Ochre for the lighter areas and more Raw Umber in the shadows.

4 Using a small natural sponge, soften brushmarks and blend the colors together. Leave gaps between the tiles.

5 If you are matching colors to an existing floor, keep standing back to compare colors (you can use the color index to help, see page 46). I needed to make the tiles more yellow to match. These tiles had a sort of ultraviolet bloom on them, made with Light Violet and white and used to exaggerate the implied light effect streaming in through imagined windows.

6 Block in the little squares with a mixture of Raw Umber, Payne's Grey and white, using more white in the lighter bits, again as if they are touched by daylight. They are lighter than you would think. The sides of these go towards the central vanishing point.

7 Finally, remove the chalk lines with a damp cloth or sponge. Using a fine pointed brush, paint the space where they were with a very dilute wash of Raw Umber and white to suggest a light-colored grout.

The Arch

My first request when planning this was that the entire room be repainted using the color 0705Y10R (a creamy, greeny, pale grey). Trompe l'oeil cannot work on a white surface as there is no room for highlights to stand out. (Look at the difference between the color inside and outside the arch).

The idea was to make the arch look like it had been built with the stone used for the fireplace on the facing wall. This meant I had something to refer to for color and texture.

An arch is the top half of an oval or ellipse, which can be drawn using Steps 1 and 2.

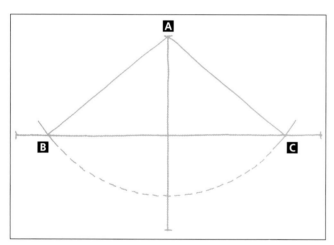

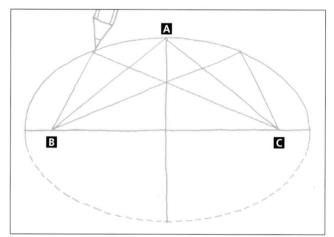

1 To draw the shape of the larger arch, first "ping" a straight horizontal line with the chalk-line starting from the point where the curve of the arch begins on one side (at the "front" of the arch) and meeting the same point on the other side. Make sure the starting points are level. This line forms the major axis (or width) of the ellipse. At right angles to the major axis and in the middle, you can draw the minor axis. Half of this is the distance from the major axis to the full height of the arch. You only use the top portion for the arch.

Open the blackboard compass to half the length of the major axis (i.e., from the middle to one end). Hold the compass steady and its point on the top of the minor axis (point A), and mark where the pencil in the compass crosses each side of the major axis. These form points B and C.

2 Next, cut a piece of string long enough to be anchored at points B and C and pulled up in the middle to reach point A, and attach the ends to points B and C with masking tape. Tuck your finger inside the loop of string and pull it round in an arc—your finger will make an ellipse which begins at the end of the major axis (i.e., the side of the arch) and meets the top of the minor axis (top of the arch). Now do the same with a pencil. Note that for the back edge of the arch (i.e., the same arch in perspective), you do exactly the same, taking the height of the top (minor axis) as if the arch were squared off as in the diagram on page 121. The starting points for the curve in perspective where the major axis sits will be found by going to the vanishing point from the same place in the full-size arch, crossing the vertical back edge of the opening.

Paints	Equipment
Burnt Sienna	Chalk line
Payne's Grey	Large school blackboard compass
Yellow Ochre	
Burnt Umber	Long piece of string
White (I used fluid acrylics which are very strong pigments in dilute form)	Masking tape
	Tape measure
	Pencil
	Compass
	Square-edged sponge (e.g., a car-washing sponge or similar), cut into pieces

3 To draw the outer arch shapes which you need for painting the stone architrave, you need an ordinary compass and a pencil. Follow the first arch shape as drawn above exactly with the needle of the compass, thus allowing the pencil to draw a replica where you want it. Adjust the compass width and repeat this several times to make the other shapes of the architrave.

4 Now you are ready to paint. All the work in this mural on the stonework was done with an ordinary square sponge, cut into fragments with one straight edge, which helped to follow the drawn guidelines. The sponge gives a gritty look to the painting. I used fluid acrylics here but I could easily have used diluted heavy body acrylics in thin washes. The colors were mixtures of Burnt Sienna, Payne's Grey, Yellow Ochre, Burnt Umber and white.

5 Build up the effect in layers, always keeping the profile of the architrave fixed in your mind, in order to be aware of the shadows and highlights.

6 White mixed with a little of the other colors is used to highlight the curves which face the light, Burnt Umber and Payne's Grey in the shadows.

7 Keep overpainting the stonework with the same colors until the texture really gives you the feeling of stone.

The Books

The books were a light-hearted trompe l'oeil exercise, with a touch of humor in the imaginary titles on the spines! Some of the titles of the books were a little far-fetched, but I had a lot of fun doing them.

The books are located in the imaginary library on fictitious shelves. Because their top and bottom edges are parallel to the direction of the viewer's feet (see page 28), these edges can be drawn using the central vanishing point on the eye-level. I attached a long piece of string to this vanishing point with masking tape (only use tape if the surface is very stable, which it should be if everything has been prepared properly, otherwise try adhesive putty), so that I could pull it out to meet the corners of the spines and easily draw the sides of the books in the correct perspective.

Paints	Equipment
Full palette of colors (see page 46)	Fine pointed sable or nylon brush
	Straight-edge (I use a piece of timber, rounded on one side, with a simple handle stuck to it—see page 38)
	Long piece of string
	8mm (⅜") flat brush

1 Start by drawing in the spines of the books in the correct position using very dilute color, a fine pointed brush and the straight edge. It's easy to wipe the paint off if you are not happy with what you've drawn, as long as you do it immediately. Look at a real bookshelf, preferably with the same sort of books on it. Notice how the edges that recede away from you follow a route towards the central vanishing point (see page 19). The spines of the books are simple shapes—like long rectangles.

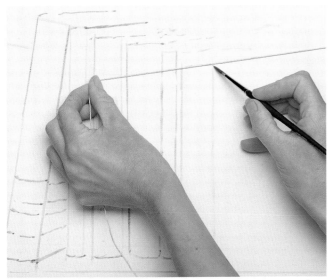

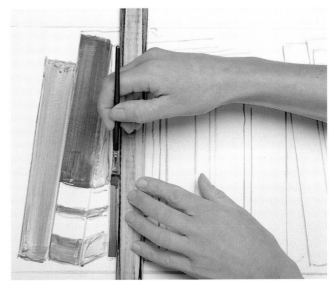

2 Attach a long piece of string to the central vanishing point (see page 19) and stretch it over to meet the tops of the spines. This helps to draw the edges which are parallel to the direction of view (in other words are parallel to the direction of your feet as you face the painting). These edges form the tops and bottoms of the sides of the books.

3 Using the straight edge as a rest for your brush (not as a masking device), start blocking in the spines and sides roughly, being as inventive as you can with colors. (You can make a straight edge with an old ruler and a couple of blobs of masking tape or adhesive putty just to keep the edge off the surface).

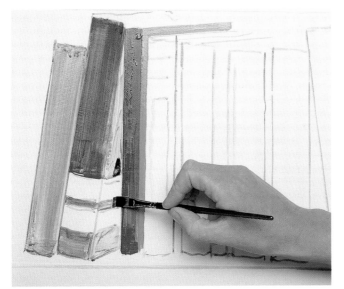

4 Keep the light source firmly in your mind, describing little shadows in between leaning books which you can spot by observation. This will begin to build depth into the painting.

5 Always make the visible tops (those below the eye-level) go towards the vanishing point. Gradually increase the detail, resorting often to observation for ideas. There is no finite version of this particular exercise. It's finished when you've had enough, but the more patience you can muster, the better the end result! By continuing to paint light and shade and all the little details on the covers you can achieve a really three-dimensional shelf of books. Then you can have fun with the lettering!

The Urn and Carrots

This urn forms part of the design I made for the same room in which I painted the Arches. Centrally positioned on the facing wall to the main mural is a beautiful French stone fireplace, from which I copied the "stonework" throughout the project. To the left of this fireplace was an empty wall ideal for a smaller painting like this, while still keeping the same theme of the "stone." An urn set into an alcove is an appealing subject because it really gives you the opportunity to play with light and shade in quite a sophisticated way. I found a reference picture of this urn in a magazine and it seemed to fit the overall style of the Arches painting.

The carrots in this mural were meant as a joke—my client had a passion for carrot juice! To help me to understand the light in this painting and paint the shadows accurately, I put the carrots inside a cardboard box on its side, arranging them so that they slightly stuck out. This simulated the light conditions which would exist if the carrots were sitting in the imagined alcove.

Fruit and vegetables are very accessible to us, so when you want to paint them, first go shopping for your subject! It might help to make drawings before you start to paint and then treat the subject as a still life.

The Carrots

Paints

Full palette of colors (see page 46)

Equipment

Fine pointed sable brush

5mm (¼") flat brush

1 First, lightly sketch the outline of the bunch of carrots with diluted Payne's Grey and white, using a fine pointed brush.

2 With a full palette of colors and a 5mm (¼") flat brush, paint directly from sight. The greens are a mixture of Jenkins Green, white, Yellow Ochre and Cadmium Yellow. The carrots are built up with mixtures of Cadmium Red, Cadmium Orange, Cadmium Yellow, Dioxazine Purple and white.

3 Continue to build depth, carefully observing all the details which help to create realism, i.e., the shadows cast by the vegetables on the surfaces around them, the roundness of each shape and the feathery fronds.

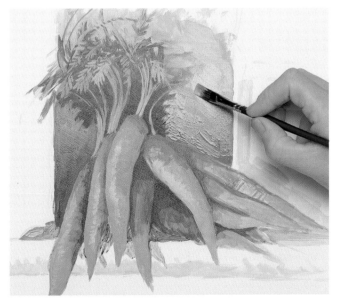

4 Keep the background abreast of the development of the vegetables—it helps to locate them in the painting. Use the flat brush for painting in the background.

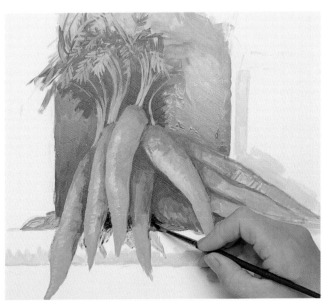

5 Using a pointed brush, put deep shadows into the spaces between the carrots to make them really sit on the shelf.

Convex Mirror

STEP-BY-STEP

Paints	Equipment
Full palette of colors (see page 46)	8mm (⅜") flat brush
	1cm (½") flat brush
	Fine pointed brush

On the right of the fireplace which faces the main mural is another space which lent itself nicely to an addition to the whole fantasy! I thought one might perhaps go through into another room opposite the "library" so I added this painting to the original concept for the whole room. Again, I used the stone architrave to "enclose" the space. I implied a light source as before, and continued the floor in exactly the same way. A focal point to which one's eye is drawn is the convex mirror, the idea for which I borrowed from a fifteenth-century painting by Van Eyck called *The Arnolfini Marriage*. In the Van Eyck painting, the backs of the betrothed couple are reflected and also another mysterious character. Mine doesn't reflect anyone, but reflects instead an imaginary room, including a fireplace just like the real one in the room "next door."

1 Start blocking in the distorted reflection with a 8mm (⅜") brush. It doesn't matter how you do this—no one will be able to tell whether it is correct or not! Just make all the straight edges bend.

2 The gilt frame was painted using a 1cm (½") flat brush and a mix of Yellow Ochre, white, Jenkins Green, Burnt Umber and Payne's Grey. When you are painting something to look gold, use a lot of deep muddy greens from which brighter, paler golden-colored highlights can glow.

3 Carry on building up detail in the reflection—the more, the merrier! I used a full palette of colors and a 8mm (⅜") flat brush to do this.

4 The floor is important and requires careful thought to make it look like a distorted version of the real floor. Add more detail with the fine pointed brush.

5 Take the fine pointed brush and add some subtle highlights to various parts of the mirror frame using white mixed with a little Cadmium Yellow to make the frame gleam.

Working to Commission

After painting several murals for yourself and your own home, you may find yourself being asked if you accept commissions from other people.

Assembling a portfolio

It's a good idea to assemble a portfolio of your work as soon as possible. Make it impressive by buying a good folder or portfolio, and taking great care to mount photographs graphically and neatly. Get some help doing this if you don't feel confident.

The way you photograph your work is extremely important. A decent camera is an invaluable tool for painting anyway, and a working knowledge of simple lighting will help not only with your painting but also in producing a good record for the folio. Avoid using a flash straight at the painting as it will "burn out" the middle. Bounced light is much better, using the ceiling or a large white reflector, which could be another wall in the room.

Without a flash, use a fast film (400 ASA) and remember that it is difficult to hand-hold a camera when using a shutter speed less than 1/60th of a second without the picture being out of focus. If you haven't got enough light, try to borrow a tripod and a cable release for the camera to minimize disturbance. Best of all, persuade an experienced friend to take the pictures for you!

Cheap film can also be a hazard. Choose a recommended brand and make sure that the film is not out of date as both these factors will affect the color quality.

Once you have started your own portfolio, keep it up to date and avoid loose photos falling out of the back of the sleeve, which is the sort of thing that detracts from your professional appearance!

Accepting a commission

If you are working for someone else and trying to arrive at a suitable fee for the job, take your time and think carefully before committing yourself. Find out from your client, if you can, how much he or she really wishes to spend before designing something that will take you a long time to paint. Your time is the main cost of the project, plus the material costs and any traveling or accommodation expenses. Your time can only be valued by you, on an hourly or daily basis. You should include in this time taken for during the preliminary design work. Having established roughly how much money is available for the work, consider how much detail you can achieve in the time paid for by that sum, making sure you also discuss at the outset who will be responsible for the other costs.

Painting takes much, much longer than other people realize, probably longer than one realizes oneself, so always err on the side of caution and add an amount that will take this into consideration. If the client takes a dim view of the cost, suggest a simpler design, rather than agreeing to do the job more cheaply. Every muralist can easily be replaced with another. You will be judged upon the basis of work that you have previously completed, your professionalism during meetings and discussions about the mural, and upon the presentation of ideas and drawings as quickly as possible after the first meeting.

At the outset, before the deal has been struck, do sketches for free (unless your reputation is of sufficiently high standing that this is not necessary). Once an idea has been agreed upon, the subject of money can be discussed and you can break the job into two parts. Firstly, the design, and secondly, the execution of the mural. You must be paid for doing a proper color design which constitutes the basis for the painting. This should form the first part of the commission itself and should be adhered to during the project, so that you know exactly what you are expected to do, and the client knows exactly what to expect. Ask for an advance payment once the commission is definite, and a letter of confirmation, agreeing on a price based on your design and any time constraints involved. Ask for either one third or one half of the whole price . Do not start work until all is settled. If you received a third in advance, then get another third once things are visibly well under way, with the balance to be paid upon completion. All this should be set out in a proper invoice. Payment upon completion means just that. It means that you have really finished the job and seen to its varnishing, hanging of panels and so on.

Other advice I can offer which might help the budding muralist on the road to success is the same sort of advice one would give to any prospective job hunter:

- Be on time for meetings.

- Be endlessly patient and helpful with suggestions and ideas for the design.

- Get your ideas down to scale on paper in a neat and well thought-out way as soon as possible, preferably in color, and always try to give your clients credit for their own ideas—even if you end up doing something completely different, they will like you for it.

- Once you have agreed on terms, order the paints and start the job. Get on with it every day and try not to become distracted by other commitments which may slow you down. Once someone has decided to have a mural, they want it finished straight away. Nothing is worse than looking at a half-painted wall.

- Be pleasant to have around so your presence will be missed later. This adds to your chances of securing the next commission.

- Take great care not to drop paint on the floor, or leave marks in the sink, and never, ever leave painted footprints anywhere in the building. Always put away your paints and tools at the end of each day.

Painting Dimensions

If you wish to reproduce any of the murals shown in this book, you can of course do so at any size. However, here are the actual sizes I painted them:

Tuscan View, page 54:
   2.5m (8') high x 1.5m (5') wide

Tabby Cat, page 64:
   life-size

Guinea Fowl, page 68:
   life-size

Cattle Murals, page 72:
   1.5m² (5' sq)

En Grisaille, page 76:
   life-size

Changing Room, page 84:
   2.8m (9') high x 5m (16') wide

The Monk, page 90:
   2.8m (9') high x 1.5m (5') wide,
   figure is life-size

A Cornish Window, page 94:
   1m (3') high x 1.2m (4') wide

The White Horses, page 100:
   main wall 2.8m (9') high x 11m (36') wide, side
   wall 2.8m (9') high x 6m (20') wide

Painted Furniture, page 112:
   approx 1m (3') high x 0.6m (2') wide

Tiepolo Mural, page 116:
   2.5m (8') high x 1.4m (4½') wide

The Arches, page 118:
   2.5m (8') high x 2.5m (8') wide,
   urn 1.5m (5') high x 1m (3') wide,
   smaller arch 2.5m (8') high x 1.2m (4') wide

Addresses

UNITED STATES AND CANADA

The paints and supplies mentioned in this book should be available at your local home improvement or craft store. Check your Yellow Pages for the location nearest you or contact any of the suppliers listed below.

Back Street, Inc.
3905 Steve Reynolds Blvd.
Norcross, GA 30093
Tel: (770) 381-7373
Fax: (770) 381-6424

CraftCo Industries, Inc.
410 Wentworth Street North
Hamilton, Ontario
Canada L8L 5W3
Website: http://www.craftco.com

Delta Technical Coatings
2550 Pellissier Place
Whittier, CA 90601
Tel: (800) 423-4135
Fax: (562) 695-5157
Website: http://www.deltacrafts.com
Acrylic, glass and fabric paints

Dick Blick Art Materials
P.O. Box 1267
695 US Highway
150 East Galesburg
IL 61402-1267
Tel: (800) 828-4548
Fax: (800) 621-8293
http://www.dickblick.com

EK Success
P.O. Box 1141
Clifton, NJ 07014-1141
Tel: (800) 524-1349
success@eksuccess.com
www.eksuccess.com
Paints and general craft products

Hobby Lobby
7707 SW 44th Street
Oklahoma City, OK 73179
Tel: (405) 745-1100
Website: http://www.hobbylobby.com

Home Depot U.S.A., Inc.
2455 Paces Ferry Road
Atlanta, GA 30339-4024
Tel: (770) 433-8211
Website: http://www.homedepot.com

Liquitex-Binney and Smith
P.O. Box 431
Easton, PA 18044-0431
Tel: (888) 422-7954
www.liquitex.com
Paints, mediums, varnishes and additives

Loew-Cornell
563 Chestnut Ave.
Teaneck, NJ 07666-2490
Tel: (201) 836-7070
Fax: (201) 836-8110
www.loew-cornell.com
Paint brushes

Lowe's Home Improvement Warehouse
Customer Care (ICS7)
Lowe's Companies, Inc.
P.O. Box 1111
North Wilkesboro, NC 28656
Tel: (800)-44LOWES
Web site: http://www.lowes.com

Michael's Arts & Crafts
8000 Bent Branch Drive
Irving, TX 75063
Tel: (214) 409-1300
Website: http://www.michaels.com

Pearl Paint
308 Canal Street
New York, NY 10013
Tel: (212) 431-7931
Website: http://www.pearlpaint.com

Pébéo of America
P.O. Box 714
Route 78, Airport Rd.
Swanton, VT 05488
Tel: (800) 363-5012
Fax: (819) 821-4151
Glass paints, markers and mediums

Silver Brush Limited
92 Main Street, Bldg. 18C
Windsor, NJ 08561
Tel: (609) 443-4900
Fax: (609) 443-4888

This book is dedicated to Derek, without whose support I could not have done it, let alone worked out how to turn the computer on… or off, for that matter!

Acknowledgments

This edition first published in North America in 2002 by North Light Books, an imprint of F&W Publications, Inc.
4700 East Galbraith Road
Cincinnati, OH 45236

First published in 2002 by New Holland Publishers (UK) Ltd
London • Cape Town • Sydney • Auckland

10 9 8 7 6 5 4 3 2 1

ISBN 1 58180 361 3

Project Editor: Gillian Haslam
Assistant Editor: Kate Latham
Photographer: John Freeman
Designer: Roger Daniels

Editorial Direction: Yvonne McFarlane

Reproduction by Modern Age Repro House Ltd, Hong Kong
Printed and bound in Singapore by Tien Wah Press (Pte) Ltd

I started running courses from my studio in Cornwall when I realized there was widespread interest in learning the art of mural painting. During the last few years it has giving me enormous pleasure to pass on what I've learnt myself from my teachers: Ken Hill, my father, mother and in particular my sister Gillian whose genius for perspective has been an absolute inspiration.

The aim of the course is to introduce trompe l'oeil to those interested in the subject by discussing basic aspects of observation, perspective, design, color and painting technique. I explain how to incorporate these skills into tackling a mural in the context of an architectural environment.

Students learn a methodical but bold and imaginative approach to painting on a large scale, while enjoying the extraordinary environment of a unique valley in Cornwall, one of the most beautiful regions of the United Kingdom.

Everyone creates a "mini mural" of their own with my help. The studio atmosphere is completely informal and fun, painting being only interrupted by wonderful, light-hearted and delicious lunches.

I have now introduced a "Level Two" two week course, by popular demand, for those wishing to extend their skills beyond the first introductory five days. Accommodation is arranged locally in a selection of recommended B&B's, all offering comfortable and friendly hospitality.

For details of my courses, please write to Janet Shearer at:
Higher Grogley Farm, Withiel, Near Bodmin,
Cornwall PL30 5NP, United Kingdom
Tel/Fax: +44 (0)1208 831 926
Email:janetshearer@macunlimited.net.
Details of paintings and courses and equipment (including Palettebox) can be found on my website: www.trompeloeil.co.uk

My friend Robert Peacop at The Paint Centre in West Drayton in Middlesex has endlessly given me advice regarding materials on request and without hesitation, and for that I am also extremely grateful as the advice he has given has been sound and reliable during difficult projects.

In recent years I am also lucky to have been supported by Jason Mackie at Global Art Supplies in London. He has promptly supplied materials of outstanding quality, both for the presentation of this book and for paintings that I have undertaken professionally and to work with such excellent paints as the Golden range of acrylics has kick-started every painting giving me the confidence to attempt almost anything!

The Consortium for Purchasing and Distribution kindly loaned the blackboard compass featured on page 40. The unpainted firescreen on page 112 was kindly given by Scumblegoosie (see suppliers) and the architect's rules were kindly loaned by the London Graphic Centre.

I'd like to thank people for whom I have painted murals for allowing them to be photographed during the writing of this book. Very special thanks to the Nare Hotel, Carne Beach, Veryan, Truro TR2 5PF, United Kingdom, Tel: +44 (0)1872 501 111, Mr and Mrs Oliver Joanes, the Watergate Bay Hotel, Watergate Bay, Nr Newquay, Cornwall TR9 4AA, United Kingdom, Tel: +44 (0)1637 860 543, Mr and Mrs Derek Jarrett, Paul and Jo Stretton-Downes, and David Bennett. Also a big thank you to Judy Lobb who helped in the nick of time to get it all finished.

Last but not least I'm indebted to Yvonne McFarlane who has given me the chance to do this book (and the computer to do it on), and to Gillian Haslam, John Freeman and Roger Daniels who helped me to understand how to!

Index

Figures in *italics* refer to figure and illustration captions